When it comes ~~to~~ ~~the issues of life,~~
God doesn't want you to be clueless.

That's why He gave you His Word. And in these pages, Bill Sanders shares with you the truths of the Bible that tell how you can deal with life's crucial questions, including:

- What's wrong with going to parties where alcohol and other drugs are offered? After all, I always say no...
- My boyfriend says either we have sex or it's over... What can I do?
- Recently one of my friends told me he was considering suicide, but then he laughed it off... Should I take him seriously?
- My father is remarried and he acts as if I don't even exist anymore. What can I do?
- How can I help my school become drug free?
- I can't control my anger. At home and at school I always blow my top and do things I regret. How can I overcome this fault?

Let *Life, Sex, and Everything in Between* clue you in on the practical, life-changing answers to these questions and lots more.

BY Bill Sanders:

Tough Turf
(Almost) Everything Teens Want Parents to Know*
  *But Are Afraid to Tell Them
Outtakes: Devotions for Guys
Outtakes: Devotions for Girls
Goalposts: Devotions for Guys
Goalposts: Devotions for Girls
Life, Sex, and Everything In Between
School Daze
Stand Tall
Stand Up
Hot & Cool: A Daily Calendar

LIFE·SEX

AND EVERYTHING IN BETWEEN

BILL SANDERS

Fleming H. Revell
A Division of Baker Book House Co
Grand Rapids, Michigan 49516

All Scripture quotations in this book are from the Holy Bible, New International Version. Copyright © 1973, 1978, 1984 International Bible Society. Used by permission of Zondervan Bible Publishers.

"Sing the Right Song," by Bill Sanders © 1990.

Library of Congress Cataloging-in-Publication Data

Sanders, Bill, date
    Life, sex, and everything in between / Bill Sanders.
      p. cm.
    Summary: Uses a question-and-answer format and a Christian perspective to approach such aspects of adolescent life as emotions, drugs, sex, friendship, and leadership.
    ISBN 0-8007-5385-2
    1. Teenagers—Religious life—Miscellanea. 2. Teenagers—Conduct of life—Miscellanea. 3. Christian life—1960– —Juvenile literature. [1. Conduct of life. 2. Christian life. 3. Questions and answers.] I. Title.
BV4531.2.S26 1991
248.8'3—dc20   90-49951
                                        CIP
                                        AC

Third printing, July 1994

Printed in the United States of America

Acknowledgments

Many people helped make this book possible. I first and foremost want to thank God for giving me this profession of working with so many young people and parents around the country. I count it a privilege to be His spokesperson to many hurting people.

Next, I would like to thank my wife. Holly, my special friend as well as wife of fifteen years, is my constant encourager and supporter. She gets the fun job of taking care of the home front and our three children while I answer more letters from desperate teens.

My secretary, Kathy Reisner, has been answering teen letters with me for the past six years. She cares for and prays for these kids as if they were her own. Her dedication in the making of and typing of this book was vitally important.

Sandy Bogema has looked over many of these answers and given me creative advice to make them stronger and more solid.

I am also very thankful for my church family at Berean. Many adults have helped me over the years in answering letters when I was on overload. Pastor Davis, Pastor Goodrich, and Pastor Kilian always have wise counsel for me when I call and say "Help!"

It's been one of my greatest pleasures over the past thirteen years to help young people around this country of ours to find hope in seemingly hopeless situations.

Contents

Introduction

Four days on the road sure make me appreciate home! No sooner had I gotten through the door than the twins and Emily clamored for attention: "Daddy, look at this! See what I can do." "Can we go play now? You promised—!" Holly, my wife, hasn't been able to get a word in edgewise. But after all the stress of being away, even this noise feels good.

Later I walk to my office, and Kathy, my priceless secretary, meets me with a handful of letters. "Bill, I think you'd better look at some of these right away." She hands me the first one, from a teen who lives with an abusive father. Suddenly my stressed-out life seems simple by comparison. As I read, my heart reaches out to a girl who needs help immediately. She's trapped in a life-or-death situation, and I must get her help— immediately. Soon the phone lines are humming, and help is on the way.

Not all the letters I get are that dramatic. "Here's one from a guy who's broken up with his girlfriend," Kathy says as she hands me one from further down in the pile. His problem won't set the phone lines humming, but he, too, needs answers, and I try to provide them.

As I tackle each of the thirty letters that came in while I was away, I agonize with each teen. Most of them have never met me, but they feel pain and need to share it. When life becomes tough, I'm glad they *can* write to tell me of their hurts—so I can offer solutions.

The answers aren't always simple—I only wish they were—

but as I sit down and answer the letters, I pour out the keys I know can open the door to a new, hopeful life. I've learned them as I've spoken in high schools, as teens have shared their troubles with me afterwards, and as they've written me to tell me their troubles.

Even though I may never speak in your school, I wanted to share these answers with you. I want you to know that everything from your personal life to your family life and school life has answers when times get tough. I've tried to provide practical, down-to-earth solutions for every teen. Use them for *Life, Sex, and Everything in Between.*

1
What Does It Mean to Be Me?

I know God loves me, but I just don't like myself. I feel so different from everyone else. What can I do?

Have you ever thought, *I don't like myself, so why should anyone else like me?* If you have, you're perfectly normal. Everyone has days when he feels down on himself or can't see why she has a best friend. When you don't like yourself, it's hard to think that someone else could love you.

When you feel different, though, realize that there's a good reason for that—you are unique. No one should be a carbon copy of anyone else. In fact, you *can't* be. Learn to be yourself—the person God created and loves.

How can you do this?

1. Accept the fact that you are unique. Being unique isn't so bad. God made you with special assets so that you can serve Him. What if everyone was good at the same thing? Everyone would want to become president, and no one would follow. God made people different so that they could do various things. Don't try to change that—you can't!

2. Stop comparing yourself with others. Since you are made unique, don't look at the most popular girl in the drama club or the best basketball player and wish to become that person. You only need to compare yourself to God. Are you becoming more like Him every day? If so, you're on the right track.

3. Look as good as you can at all times. How you look can have a strong impact on how you feel. That doesn't mean you have to have the latest brand-name clothes and spend thousands of dollars on a wardrobe, but don't dress as if your wardrobe came from a garbage can.

If you get hung up on what you wear by comparing yourself to others, you won't find happiness. Just make certain you're the best *you* can be, and you'll feel better inside.

4. Help less fortunate people. To stop feeling sorry for yourself, become a Big Sister or a Big Brother. Visit the juvenile home, help out with Youth for Christ, or become active in another people-oriented area. Then you can appreciate the things you have.

5. Develop positive character qualities. Instead of becoming hung up on what you wear or what group you're in, develop positive character qualities such as honesty, integrity, and perseverance. Show people they can count on you, and good friends will find you.

6. Never give in to wrong. If you're doing wrong, you will feel bad about yourself. Keep your life open to God by following His

Word, the Bible, and seeking to know Him better. If others encourage you to sin, don't be afraid to say no or lose their friendship; you don't need friends who don't want the best for you.

7. Make the best of your strong points. By not comparing yourself with others, you free yourself to become the best you can in the things that interest you. Discover the hobbies you enjoy: Do you want to learn to play the violin, play squash, or sail? What things make you happy when you do them? Take them on!

8. Call yourself a chooser, not a loser. Develop your ability to make decisions. Try out new things or carefully think out new situations, so you can make the best choice. Throughout your life you're going to have to make decisions. Make them wise ones.

9. Make the best choice. If you only make one decision in life, accept Jesus as your Savior. Open your heart to Him, and all things become possible. He can give you the strength you need to make right choices, the power to say no to sex, and the knowledge that you are special in His eyes.

10. Give Him your life and worries. When troubles come up, you need not carry them alone. Jesus, your Friend, wants to help you through them. But you have to make that possible by trusting Him, no matter what!

11. Believe that God loves you. Don't just say it; learn to mean it. Make your actions live up to your words by putting that truth in your life-style. Study His Word. Read Psalm 139 to learn how special you are to Him and how He cares for you every moment.

You told us to be glad that we are who we are and to use our talents, but I always seem to compare myself with others. What should I do?

I think I can best express this through the following poem.

Be Glad You're You

I want to be me.
Please want to be you.
To ourselves and God
we can both be true.

Don't want my gifts;
I won't want yours.
Thank God for your strengths,
and you'll please Him for sure.

It saddens our Lord
when we always compare,
too busy pleasing others
to love and to share.

He waits for compassion
or an uplifting phrase.
God is before us
in His mysterious ways.

He is the kid who is not cool
and has no friends at school.

He is the girl no one calls on the phone
or who watches movies all alone.

14

If we're too busy comparing,
there is no time for sharing,
and we all stop caring.

Then I'm not me,
and you're not you,
and to ourselves
we're never true.

Let's say no more.
Let's start today,
to see ourselves
in a special way.

God made us unique
with whatever it takes.
Be assured of this:
HE MAKES NO MISTAKES.

You're you for a reason,
and that reason is true.
Today more than ever
Let God shine through you.

Start out by caring
and helping someone.
Then honor the Lord,
when you're having fun.

All that you do
turn over to Him.
You'll never feel worthless
or useless within.

I'm glad I'm me.
Be glad you're you.
Live for the Lord.
Nothing better can you do.

My family never seems to have a good word to say about me. They always compare me with my older brother. Sometimes I don't think even God could love me!

Though it's easy for parents to pick one child and turn him into an example for the whole family, hearing that sibling praised all the time and never hearing about your own good points can hurt. But instead of falling into bad habits because of it, overcome this situation.

1. Remember that God really *does* love you. He always has and always will. Because of the way your family treats you and how you view them, you may not feel very loved, but that can change.

If you wait for your family to approve of you, you may become frustrated. Until things improve, focus on your heavenly Father, who sent His Son, Jesus, to die for you. Appreciate the love He has given you—love far greater than you'll find in any earthly family.

2. Talk to your brother. Don't be angry at him. After all, he has not made your parents act this way. Ask if he has noticed it, how he feels about it, and what suggestions he has. Maybe he will go to your parents with you.

3. Talk to your parents or write them a letter. Tell them how much you perceive that they compare you with your brother. Share your good points with them, the strengths, desires, goals, and talents you have that are missing in your brother. While you do so, though, do not attack your brother.

4. Be yourself. God made you different from your brother for a reason. Don't change to fit your parents' hopes and perceptions. In the long run, that cannot make you or them happy. Seek out the things God has for *you,* the unique person He created.

5. Develop good life skills. Show your parents your honesty, gentleness, compassion, and ability to work hard. Don't let the situation make you bitter and deprive you of the desire to relate well to others.

6. Tell your parents that you need their love. Tell them you need their total, unconditional acceptance and love. Let them know how much that will mean to you.

7. Explain the influence they have on you. Tell your mom and dad that how they parent you will mold the way you grow and what type of parent you become. Ask them if they want you to pass on these feelings to future grandchildren.

8. Forgive them. Your mom and dad probably don't realize that they have gotten into such a bad habit or that it hurts you so much. Doubtless they are doing their best to raise you well. Don't let their weakness ruin you. Keep negative emotions from harming you by making forgiveness a habit.

9. Depend on God. With His help you can overcome this. When times seem tough, turn to your heavenly Father for strength. Even through your pain He can mold you into a more compassionate person—if you don't let hate and bitterness tie you down.

When I have to make a tough choice, how can I know I am making the right decision?

As a teen, you can face tough decisions every day. During these years you begin to discover truths about yourself and life and the good and bad things they hold.

Whatever action you choose, first ask yourself the following questions:

1. Does it violate one of God's rules? If it does, it will always be wrong. People may tell you it's okay to lie, cheat, or steal, but God says no! No matter what anyone claims, that will never change. If you *do* decide to go against His rules, you *will* pay the price.

Save yourself a lot of heartache by searching the Bible to discover the advice God's Word has for you. If God says yes, then do it; if He says no, then don't. He gave you those guidelines to help you avoid lots of pain.

If you can't find the answers in your Bible, why not ask some-one else whom you respect where to find the answer? Your pastor, youth leader, or a Sunday-school teacher may be able to turn you to the right verses and show you what they mean.

2. Does this action violate one of man's laws? God's Word doesn't say anything about speeding, but that doesn't mean it's okay. Our government makes laws for our good, and God wants us to obey them.

Only consider disobeying a man-made law when it disagrees with God's Word. For example, our laws say a woman has the right to abort an unborn baby, and the government will pay for it. But God's Word makes it clear we are living human beings with fingerprints and heartbeats when we are still inside our mothers' wombs. In such a case a Christian needs to do what's right, not seek out legal rights that don't agree with God's truths.

3. Am I on the wrong road? What if God's Law isn't black and white on an issue? When it doesn't spell out what you should do, remember this little ditty: "If God's rules aren't black or white, will it lead me toward wrong or right?" For example, God's Word does not specify what you should do on a date. Nowhere does it say, "Thou shalt not go parking or kiss passionately." But if gray areas like those could lead you to actions you'd regret, it's better to bypass that parking place and hold back on the kissing. Be wise and smart. Don't get started down the wrong road.

When a gray area tempts you, ask yourself, *What are my chances of going farther and regretting my actions?* If there is any chance at all, run. It takes real courage to get out of Dodge City when a gunslinger walks the street, seeking to make you a notch on his pistol.

4. Whose advice can I ask? If you have trouble making a decision, seek out the advice of a wiser, older person who has your best interests at heart.

You'll hear music that advises you to have a good time, and friends may encourage you to do things you'd rather bypass. To tune in to what's right, seek out the opinion of someone who has a good track record when it comes to decision making. Ask your parents, older friends, teachers you respect, or a minister or counselor. When that person gives you advice, listen to it carefully and consider putting it into action.

5. What are the long-term results? Will this cause fun in the short run, but pain for the rest of your life—or even just a long time? If so, say no. Don't choose to play now, pay later. Do you need to spend your life as a single parent, living in poverty, because you made an unwise choice today? No, make the better decision.

6. What is my long-term plan? If emotions catch you up, you can make a bad, spur-of-the-moment decision. Plan ahead and follow your plan. It's never too late to say no to premarital sex, but when you're half undressed on the couch, it may be hard to convince your date you mean business.

Follow the *best* plan. Instead of going to a party where there are drugs and planning on not taking them, plan never to go. Tell your date or friends you won't go certain places. Stick by the things you know are good and avoid those that cause harm: premarital sex, pornography, alcohol or drugs, stealing, cheating, and so on.

Ask yourself, *What is good for me and others?* Your future, your friends, and your family all deserve your best. Don't let inconsiderate planning hurt people.

Before you make a tough decision, go over these questions in your mind. Begin forming habits that will develop your character. Become the person God wants you to be, not a wishy-washy one swayed by the thoughts of others.

Would you feel embarrassed, dirty, or bad doing this activity, if God or your parents were standing by you as you did it? If so, I think you know what to do.

You talk about honesty and truly being honest to ourselves. How can we know if we are really honest?

I found a simple solution through a book called *Honest to God?* by Bill Hybels. It has inspired and guided me. From this book I learned that when I'm really honest with God, I'm honest with myself and everyone else. A true honesty means who we are when we are all alone, not just when people are looking at us and we try to shine for our popularity's sake and our reputation. I've tried to express it in a poem.

Honest to God

Honest to God, and others, too,
that's what I want to be:
When I'm truly honest to God,
then I'm honest with me.

I've performed in front of you,
   to make me look real good.
But Jesus taught me yesterday
   how to do what I should.

God is my one, eternal Judge
   and my most awesome Friend.
Instead of pleasing all the world,
   I'll live for Him instead.

I used to say "honest to God,"
   to make my words sound true,
but being really honest means
   I am that way with you.

I like the man in the mirror,
   because I've changed my ways,
and now I know, beyond a doubt,
   honest to God does pay.

Not in the ways I used to think—
   look great or act so cool—
when I'm truly honest to God,
   to Him I am no fool.

Honest with God, and deep inside,
   I quietly can hear
God's extraspecial messages
   and know when they are near.

First meet Him, then become honest,
   of joy you'll not be robbed.
Then keep in your heart this promise:
   Be truly honest to God.

As I've said many times before, in all of my books, I challenge you. The greatest thing you can do is to recognize that you do need your Creator and that a long, long time ago, God sent Jesus to the cross to die for our sins. He honestly loved us the greatest way He knew how, by sending His only beloved Son to give up His life so we could live with Him forever. Today be honest with God and yourself. Don't be ashamed of the God who sent His Son to die for you. Turn your life over to Him; let Him live through you. It works, honest!

At school some of the things I learn— about sex, drinking, what college I should go to, and whom I should date—don't agree with what I hear at home and in church. Am I on another planet? How can I decide what's right for me?

Do you go to a public school that teaches situational ethics (they may call it values clarification)? If so, in the classroom your teacher may explain that sometimes a thing is right, and other times it's wrong. "If it doesn't hurt someone," he may have said, "it's probably right for that time."

Meanwhile, you'd be afraid to tell your Sunday-school teacher what he said; she'd probably faint! No wonder you feel as if you were on a different planet.

For example, your parents taught you that lying is wrong. At school they'll tell you it's okay. "After all," someone in your class argues, "don't good things sometimes come out of lying? It can even help people or cause good things to happen." You hardly know what to believe.

Today you probably have a better chance at seeing the moon turn into cheese than you do of hearing a teacher publically say, "Right is right, and wrong is wrong. It will never be right to do wrong." But that doesn't mean that right and wrong don't exist.

Let's look specifically at the things you mentioned.

Sex is definitely right for you—*if* you are with the right person, in the right situation. That means after you marry and only with your spouse.

Despite what your teachers may tell you, you can easily see that "safe sex" isn't all it's cracked up to be. Look at three ways you can feel pain when you take part in sex outside of marriage:

> *Physically:* Sex with someone other than your spouse could give you a sexually transmitted disease: herpes, gonorrhea, syphilis—or AIDS. AIDS can lie dormant in a person's body for as long as fifteen years. Today you may not know anyone who has it, but will you be able to say that in fifteen years? How many of your old friends will be dying from it?
> *Emotionally:* When you have sex and get dumped, you feel awful. It starts to affect your whole life, because your self-worth has dropped into the gutter. You look for someone to make you feel better—a sex partner—and you start the cycle all over again. You can't feel good about yourself under those circumstances.
> *Spiritually:* Once you start having sex, you become so addicted that you will lie or do anything else to get it. The longer you go against God's will, the farther you drift away from Him.

There is no right way to have sex outside of marriage. Sure, people will tell you how wonderful it is, but if you could see inside them, you'd feel the pain they have from those failed relationships. Do you want to make a decision that leads to that? Who would plan for such a heartache?

How about alcohol? Is it right for you? If you're under age, drinking's illegal. The people who tell you it's okay still cannot change the law. At one point some states tried lowering the drinking age—and paid the price in increased alcohol-related deaths. How did the government respond? They raised the drinking age again! Those who tell you drinking is okay cannot return to life the people who died so that some teens could drink. Even if it weren't illegal, do you want to take the risk that you'll be one of the six out of ten people who have problems in life—sometimes directly related to alcohol use.

When you try to decide what college to go to, you need to make many choices. Is going to college right for you? Do you have the desire to go? If you want to, you should go.

What college should you pick? Make your choice carefully. Think it through.

I went to a very liberal school. No one taught me right from wrong, and I was never challenged to turn my life over to God or live in a way that would please Him. Never once did a teacher inspire me to live with integrity. Though I got my degree, while I was there I also learned "if it feels good, do it" and "society rules." I didn't discover those were not good rules for life until after I left school.

Whatever college you pick, realize that you will learn many lessons that have nothing to do with your classes or books. Choose a school that will give you good opportunities, not a life-style you will come to regret. Make your decision wisely, knowing you will never stop learning.

You also need to choose wisely when you date. If you believe in the Lord Jesus, is it right for you to seriously date someone who does not? Perhaps you could win her over, but you must also face the possibility that she will win *you* over to her way of life. Will you fall in love with a guy who does not believe in right and wrong, and get badly hurt in the process? Why take the chance of falling in love with and marrying someone who does not share your faith?

People who live by situational ethics keep running into bad situations. As long as they cannot take into account the long-term evils of poor choices they will have to live with the results of a life that has no firm moral standards. Why choose that, when you can have blessings? Stick to right, and you won't have a wrong life.

School's so boring. What can I do to make it more exciting?

I'm glad you asked this question, because there *is* something you can do to improve every day. You don't have to get in trouble, do drugs, or hang with a tough crowd to have a good time.

1. Start by planning how you will get through the day. Decide to do something different. Make someone else feel wanted, special, or needed. Sit next to a lonely student in the cafeteria. Make a new friend. Pick up a paper you didn't drop. Ask a teacher what you can do to help. Really have fun in everything you do by not comparing your looks, clothes, or abilities with anyone else's.

2. In class, make up some goals for good grades. Become involved in learning. Ask well-thought-out questions. If you have trouble in a class, get a tutor. Once you understand a subject, it becomes more fun.

3. Make activities part of your schoolday. Get involved in sports, vocational groups, the debating team, the drama group, or student government; take part in jobs like library aide or office help. Discover an area you are interested in, and get involved. Make it *your* school. Don't blame others if you don't become part of what's going on.

4. Learn effective study techniques. There are many ways to study well. Find better ways to write term papers or study for tests. Ask a better student for guidelines.

By finding something new and constructive to do, you won't have time to feel bored.

I am a guy who's having a hard time figuring out the difference between being macho and soft. I love my family, but I don't want to be a sissy. What does it really mean to be tough in today's world?

Your question inspired me to write a poem. I've just poured my heart into this and I do believe that I was blessed by the words that came out. I hope that this answers your question, gives you the idea that you can have emotions, and shows you what the word *tough* really means.

Big Boys Do Cry

We've heard it all our lives,
but now we are hard, insensitive,
don't know our kids or wives.

Big boys do cry.
Macho ain't enough.
Tenderness adds to life,
more than being tough.

A stiff upper lip
was desired long ago,
but we couldn't cry,
and when asked why,
no one seemed to know.

Emotions were for sissies,
girls and little boys.
Real men grow, fight, and cuss
and play with big boys' toys.

But cry? No way!
It shows how weak you are.
Be strong and in control,
or you'll never be the star.

But look at men.
They know not where to hail.
The macho type is mean and tough;
the effeminate is frail.

God planned for more
on the eve of man's start.
That's why He gave each of us
a wonderful, loving heart.

Sissy or sassy
which way is best?
God shed His mercy
to give us tenderness.

But if we were not tough,
and dominating fools,
wouldn't others say
we know not how to rule?

I doubt it,
because, more than ever before,
the world is desperate
for men tough enough to soar.

Be tough enough to pray to God
and with your friends at meals
and buckle up before you drive,
don't brag about your wheels.

Tough enough to tell your mom
what others fear to do.
Hug her, hold her,
Then say, "I love you."

Tough enough to say,
"I'm sorry, I was wrong,"
Tough enough to write a poem
or sing a lovely song.

Tough enough to tell your girl,
"We're both worth waiting for.
I won't use you;
You don't use me;
and God will keep the score."

Tough enough to get married
and be a dad someday
and when trouble comes—
Divorce? No way!

With God's help
we'll work it out.
Right here
is where we'll stay.

Tough enough to always
devote himself to God
in memorizing Scripture,
not working on his bod.

Yet tough enough to eat what's right
and work out if it's hot
and caring much for others—
never put them on the spot.

You're not macho or hard
or soft like lard.
You care, that's why we share,
and to the end, we'll be there.

If you are hurting
and need a friend.
We're tough enough to pray for you
to the better end.

Now that you've read this, I hope you realize what it *really* means to be tough. Do you have the courage to do the right thing, when others can't? Do you have the strength to be tender? That's true toughness.

Be proud of both the things you believe in and your strengths. Never fear telling those you love about that emotion. Saying, "I love you," shows your marvelous inner strength. God bless you!

People are always getting on my case about being Miss Perfect. What's so wrong with being a perfectionist? I inherited this trait from my dad.

Being a perfectionist is a tough way to go through life. Sure, you like to get things done right, and that's great. But what happens when things *aren't* perfect? Do you feel as if you can't try something if you can't do it well? Do you avoid people who don't fit with your perfect image? That's pretty limiting.

Perfectionists fear taking risks. They seldom raise their hands if they suspect they might have the wrong answer or if someone else might make fun of them. They fear going on a trip, unless they know no one will take any risks and all will go smoothly. Their friends always admire their, oh, so neat houses. But inside, perfectionists have stress and fear. They may avoid going outside in anything less than the most perfect outfit, because they want to look right at all times.

We've all heard the expression "practice makes perfect," and some of us believe that more than others. Vince Lombardi added to that, saying, "Perfect practice makes perfect." Well, I'd like to challenge those statements. To prove that practice has not, does not, and never will make perfect, I offer you this thought: Do you know anyone who *is* perfect at anything? Do you know someone who has practiced a musical instrument for years and never makes a mistake on it? I don't. Do you know an athlete who performs perfectly in his or her sport? I don't either. Practice can make better—to a point—but it never makes us perfect. Remember this instead, "Practice makes permanent."

Counselors will tell you they most often see the people who

try to be perfect, not only in cleaning the house, but in relationships and life itself. These counselors seek to give them a better mental balance.

Less often counselors see the folks who can laugh, joke, go to the mall in grubby clothes, and not worry about their hairstyles. Though they lack perfection, the "imperfectionists" are very healthy mentally and emotionally. People are not perfect; we *all* goof up.

When I meet with mothers who want their housework perfect, I suggest, "Let the house go for a couple of months."

They start to sweat, grab their collars, and think, *I could never do that!* Right beside them sit mothers thinking, *We're doing it right! We're doing it right!*

Thank God for the ability He gave you to want to do things right. You are probably organized and levelheaded—and those are wonderful qualities. But lighten up on your perfectionism by remembering that any strength, overused, becomes your greatest weakness. Keep in balance. Have fun, too.

People pick on me because I have asthma. I don't know how to deal with it. Please help!

To deal with this, you'll have to learn to make your weakness your strength. Don't apologize; this is you. You don't have to feel all sorry for yourself or for the way your body is.

Find friends who accept you for who you are. These are the people really worth getting close to. With their help and support, you will find it easier to confront those who pick on you.

When kids make fun of you, that is their problem, not yours. Even though their words hurt, ignore them. Don't let others' meanness determine how you act. Instead, respond in love and kindness. You will win them over, in time, through your courage and compassion. As you do, you will make friends who really admire you for who you are and not what they can get from you.

Believe it or not, you may find that your weakness is a blessing in disguise. When you respond to others in love, you will develop character qualities that might otherwise never have become a part of you. You'll know your true friends, too.

Be thankful you are who you are and let God and your special friends help you become the best person possible.

I'm fourteen years old. One day, when my friend was at my house, some older boys came over and tried to get us to smoke crack. We didn't know how to tell them to leave, so we locked ourselves in my bedroom. They yelled for a while, but finally they left. They broke some things in our house and left it a mess. What should I do?

You were in a potentially dangerous situation. In America we often think bad things only happen to bad people—it would never happen to us—but you know better, because it came so close to you.

I believe these guys think of you as an easy mark—someone with little or no ability to resist them. Though you probably let them in, you didn't feel comfortable asking them to leave. They seemed too old, too big, or too powerful. Maybe you didn't have the nerve to call 911.

Crack is cocaine, and when a person is on it, he does not know who he is or what is going on, and quite often he will do things he won't remember later. At the very least, he can act in a way he will regret for a very long time.

If these boys came into your home, not caring when your parents would return, they are very reckless. Obviously they don't care about their bodies, and they don't care about yours, or they wouldn't try to get you to use crack. They are breaking the law by taking this drug, so they probably would break it with other activities as well. Why take the chance of having these boys come in again and rape you or harm you in another way that will last a lifetime? Don't take a chance at letting them through the door, since they could drop another drug into a drink without your knowing, and you could die from an overdose.

Talk to your parents. Call the police. Do something about it. It is time that people who use drugs, sell them, and push them get caught. Though you may feel like a narc, realize that these boys need help. If you don't want anyone to know, do it anonymously. Often such people will thank you in the end for getting them the help they need. America's jails and prisons are filled with those who didn't have caring individuals who shouted out their names to the authorities. A person who takes drugs is crying out for help. When no one picks up on the cries, he may do something stupid or cause someone else lasting pain.

If you don't feel comfortable about going to your local police or your parents, go to your counselor. Talk to an adult who cares. Tell someone, because this has to be dealt with. Since you only have fourteen years of experience, you can't know the dangerous or fatal things that could happen in such a situation. Be smart and do something before someone gets hurt.

As a teenager, what can I do to make sure I'm never kidnapped or abducted?

You may think this problem only touches babies or little children, but hundreds of times each year teens disappear, and no one sees them again. Being prepared can protect you from the sick, hurting people in the world who could harm you if they had the right chance, at the right time.

1. Whenever possible, give your parents an idea of where you plan to be. It's not a sissy thing to keep in touch. You don't have to call them wherever you stop, just make certain they have an idea about your plans. Are you going to a mall with friends or going to a party with the team? Your parents care what happens to you, but if they have no idea where you are, you could easily disappear without a trace.

2. Go most places in groups. Numbers can scare off a kidnapper or murderer. Sure, you may still be approached when you're in a group, but the odds are greater that it won't happen.

3. Don't talk to or approach strangers. Do you and your friends stray in public places? Would you go off alone with a stranger? Be aware that those are dangerous habits. Many lost young people were seen for the last time walking alone or with a friend in a mall. Once they reached dark areas, they became easy prey.

4. Beware of anyone who promises you something. Though teens should be able to see through this, they often don't. Never let greed or desires lead you to take a wrong step. The person who promises you something if you just go off with him expects something in return.

5. Avoid staying at home alone. Many kidnappers know that parents work and leave young people at home alone. An inexpensive lock on the front door cannot match wits with a creative, deceptive person twice the size of his human victim. If you *are* alone and a stranger comes to the door, don't open it. If he doesn't go away, call the police!

6. When you go out, arrange for a ride home ahead of time. Make certain it's a *safe* ride. If at all possible, have your parents pick you up on time. If you need to wait, do so in a crowd or inside. Don't stay alone at school once the adults have gone. Should your parents be late, ask a teacher, principal, or the coach to remain a few minutes until your mom or dad comes.

If your parents can't pick you up, make certain you ride home with a friend—someone you know you can trust. Don't allow anyone to push you into taking a ride with a person you've never met before. How can you tell what you're getting into?

Whatever happens, don't just figure, *I can handle it*. Precautions will keep you safe. If you're suddenly alone with someone you don't know, and a chill creeps up your spine, you may realize, too late, that you've made a big mistake. I don't want you to have to go through that.

Protect yourself from someone who might sexually molest you—or kill you—by taking these simple steps. I don't want to read your sad story in the papers someday!

I'm eighteen and about to graduate. I'm kind of scared, thinking of my future. Any advice?

Life has begun to change for you. Now you face new decisions, and it's perfectly normal to feel nervous. When you feel overwhelmed, don't get down. Look at what you have going for you.

1. You can put your trust in God. He loves you and wants to help you through this time. If you pray, asking Him for guidance, He will show you the way. Remain close to Him by acting in His will, as far as you know it, instead of rebelling from church and all it stands for.

2. Realize who loves you most. In addition to God, you have your parents, special friends, and the adults you look up to. Because they have wisdom and experience, make use of their advice. Their knowledge could save you some expensive mistakes. Ask what they think about college, your career, and where you should live. Listen carefully to their ideas.

3. Look at the past. You were probably scared when you went from third grade into fourth grade, but it went fine. Focus on past successes. All through life you'll face new challenges and change. Millions of others have done it, and you can, too.

4. Look to the future. When you ask questions, you show wisdom and common sense. Recognize potential problems before you face them. Then you can proceed with a mixture of caution and confidence. Don't fear risk, and be creative. Act with character and confidence, and you won't regret it!

Do you have any regrets in your own life?

More than you'll ever know, I regret the times I've made myself more important than God, my family, and others. I regret any times I've hurt my wife, Holly, and my kids. I think of my parents and some really close friends I've lost over the years. And of course there are times when I've hurt my Best Friend, Jesus.

Sin sticks to your mind like glue. Though I know my Creator and Savior has forgiven me, those memories will always remain.

Shortly before my dad died, I asked him what things he wished he had done in his lifetime. Quickly yet sadly, he replied, "It's not those things I think about, these days. It's all the things I wish I *hadn't* done." He knew the haunting memories of regret.

But life doesn't have to be filled with regrets. You can walk close to God, doing things His way. Seek right more than gratification. Put good, healthy memories in your mind.

Want to avoid regrets? Before you do something, ask yourself:

1. Does it look good in God's eyes? Look at it from His viewpoint. Does this go against what He has said in the Scriptures? Will it draw you closer to Him? If not, give yourself the gift of good memories by taking another path—one of which He will approve.

2. Am I motivated to lead others closer to God? What motivation lies behind your action? Are you doing a "good" thing for the wrong reason? Make certain you are not simply seeking your own pleasure, but put the good of others first.

3. Will it lead someone away from God? Does this action create a poor testimony to those around you? Will it make a fellow Christian stumble, or will someone decide Christians are bad because of your act? If so, say no!

4. Do I think about others? Don't consider only yourself. If it would hurt someone needlessly, don't do it. What kind of impact will it have on the life of those with whom you have contact?

5. Whom will this help? Is this action going to benefit others? You cannot avoid regret if you harm the friends, family, and God who support you. If you cannot take them into consideration, I doubt you want to take this action.

6. Am I doing the best I can? Don't settle for second or third best in your life. If it's not in your best interest, find another way.

(But *best* doesn't always mean "perfect." Don't let fear keep you from doing something because you might not perform as well as someone else. Just do it the best *you* can.)

I've heard you speak several times, and you've always touched my heart. I noticed you always work God into each message. Why?

When I speak, I don't work at mentioning God; in fact I don't even think about it. He's so much a part of my life that I simply share Him when I share from the heart. It's very natural.

Not a day goes by that I don't think of the broken-down wreck I was before God got ahold of my life. Before I knew Him, my marriage was on the edge of ruin, and most of my friends had left me because I'd been so selfish. I felt severely depressed and even attempted suicide. Because I was a liar and cheat, I didn't like myself.

When God's love filled me, through His Son, Jesus Christ, I became a new person. He did so much for me that I have a hard time conceiving of telling teens how special they are without telling them about their Creator. It's impossible for me to talk to a depressed high-school senior without telling him about the reason I have hope in my own life.

In very few places have I had trouble mentioning my faith. I speak of it very tactfully, and people usually appreciate my sincerity. I work hard on understanding their beliefs and feelings. Every time I speak, I pray for each member of the audience.

When I'm talking I tell them I prayed for them and want their pain to stop.

If that's working God in, I guess I do it.

I believe in God, do my best, and try to go to church as much as possible. Doesn't that mean I'm a Christian?

Knowing God is so much more than making a list of rules to follow or walking inside church doors as often as you can. I want you to know God as a Person and live with Him forever. If you don't already know Him that way, you can, if you:

1. Realize that you have sinned. The Bible says, ". . . all have sinned and fall short of the glory of God" (Romans 3:23). Have you ever known someone who never made a mistake, goofed up, or fell short of God's perfection? I haven't. Each of us has sinned against God; we have goofed up some way and need His help. We need to realize that we have a need for a Savior.

Tell God you are not perfect and you need Him.

2. Recognize that God has the solution. Jesus Christ, God's only Son, died for our sins, so we could enter into God's presence sinless and stainless. The Bible tells us: "But God demonstrates his own love for us in this: While we were still sinners, Christ died for us" (Romans 5:8). It also says, "For God so loved the world that he gave his one and only Son, that whoever believes in him shall not perish but have eternal life" (John 3:16).

It's as if we were on one side of a canyon, with our sins, and God were on the other side. A large valley lies between us. On our own, we could never jump to Him, climb down, or fly over the space. To get us from one side to the other, Jesus Christ would have to stretch His body across, so we could walk over on Him.

In John 14:6, Jesus warned, "I am the way and the truth and the life. No one comes to the Father except through me." To get to the Father, we have to walk across that space on Jesus. Nothing else will do.

3. Know that doing good can never save you. No matter how often you go to church, you can never get into heaven on that act. "For it is by grace you have been saved, through faith—and this not from yourselves, it is the gift of God—not by works, so that no one can boast" (Ephesians 2:8, 9).

Giving money, doing work for the church, or being as good as we can, cannot pave our way to heaven. Only faith in Jesus can do that.

4. Accept the fact that you can't pay for eternal life. God gives it to us for free: "For the wages of sin is death, but the gift of God is eternal life in Christ Jesus our Lord" (Romans 6:23). Death is the payoff for sinning, but God gives us a choice. We can have His gift. We pay nothing to receive Him, but once He's in our hearts He will mean more than popularity, pride, people, wealth, fame, or beauty. Make Him your Lord today.

5. Say it and mean it. ". . . If you confess with your mouth, 'Jesus is Lord,' and believe in your heart that God raised him from the dead, you will be saved. For it is with your heart that you believe and are justified, and it is with your mouth that you confess and are saved. . . . 'Everyone who calls on the name of the Lord will be saved' " (Romans 10:9, 10, 13).

On Christmas Day, 1978, I recognized my sins, felt sorry for them, and understood that only faith in Christ could admit me to the sinless presence of God. I prayed, "Dear Lord, I am sorry for all my sins. I'm sorry for the way I've hurt You and others. I know I've done wrong and want to be forgiven.

"I have faith in You, Jesus, and I want You to help me clean up my life. Come into my life and be my Lord and Savior. Be my strength and wisdom and courage in knowing what to do—help me know the difference between right and wrong.

"The Bible says You died for my sins and rose from the dead. I believe it, and I believe You when You say that if I believe in Your name I shall be saved eternally. Amen."

That was a long time ago, and I can tell you beyond any doubt that God has never left me. Many times I've left Him and questioned Him, but He has never left my heart.

When I asked Jesus into my heart, I didn't have a revelation or hear God speaking from the skies. I never spoke in another language, and my hair didn't turn another color, but I felt His peace in my heart. I saw Him restore my marriage, my friendships, my profession, and my dignity.

If you ask Jesus into your heart, He'll do the same kinds of things in your life. Say the prayer I prayed, and believe in Him. Then never let anyone tell you you are not really saved. By having faith, you have Jesus.

If you have accepted Jesus as a result of reading this, fill out the form in the back of the book and send it to me. I have some materials for you that will help you grow in the Lord.

Your response to God's offer is the greatest decision you will ever make. Jesus will take you, whatever shape you are in, with all your troubles, pains, addictions, or frustrations. He wants to be your Strength, Guide and Best Friend.

As He knocks on the door of your heart, please open up and let Him in.

2
Why Do I Feel This Way?

I feel so lonely. I never know what to do when I feel this way, and I'm tired of feeling down and out. I need some help. I need a friend. Please help!

Feeling lower than a snake's navel isn't fun. No one wants to stay down in the dumps for long, but every perfectly normal person does have days like these. So don't worry if it happens once in a while.

That doesn't mean you have to stay depressed, that you can't make a friend, or that you're doomed to remain lonely for the rest of your life. Understand what it means to be lonely and how to get out of this emotion.

1. What does it mean to be lonely? Being alone and loneliness are two different things. Everyone wants some time to himself, time to slow down, relax, and order his life. Can you think of times when you've been happy to spend time alone? How about times when you couldn't wait to get off by yourself?

Have you ever felt lonely in a crowd? That usually happens because you feel that no one there truly cares for you. But if a friend walks in and begins to talk to you, your whole perspective may change. Suddenly you feel part of things again. When you feel lonely, look for an unmet need in you that needs caring for.

2. Loneliness may have a simple cause. If you've been in a troubled or stressed situation, or if you just confronted something you've never handled before, you may feel lonely. Perhaps you've just had a fight with your best friend. By identifying the cause of your feelings and acting to correct a trouble spot, you may solve your problems and begin to feel better fast.

3. Loneliness can consume you. If you feel lonely and don't take steps to get rid of it, that emotion can overwhelm you. Instead of falling into the loneliness habit, fight back. Don't slip into the cycle of sadness: *take action!* You'll be surprised how quickly that will change how you feel.

Loneliness doesn't have to remain, if you take a few simple steps:

1. Avoid compromise. While you feel down in the dumps, don't set aside your beliefs, values, and the things that are important to you. To keep from feeling lonely, girls have had sex outside of marriage—and ended up regretting it. In seeking intimacy, don't give away something precious. Nor should you take drugs, become involved in crime, or lie, cheat, and steal to achieve popularity. In the long run, you'll only do yourself great harm. Avoid regrets by avoiding compromise.

2. Become active. When you feel lonely because a friend whom you've hurt avoids you, if your pride stands between you and the phone call that could heal that friendship, push aside your pride. Be humble enough to ask for forgiveness.

Whatever the issue that keeps you apart, confront it. Until you do, you will feel little peace.

3. Think of your old friends and make new ones. When have you really felt close to someone? Take yourself back to a time when you and your friend shared something that brought you joy and didn't hurt either of you. Bring back those memories and see what made that friendship work.

Make Jesus your Best Friend. Once He comes into your heart, you never need to be lonely again. No matter what you go through, no matter how many—or few—friends you have, He will always stay by your side. Don't turn from the chance to be God's friend.

Not only will Jesus become your Friend, He can show you the best way to build human friendships. To draw close to others, you need to love yourself and them, and love comes from God. You might say it works in a cycle:

Cut God out of the picture, and that cycle becomes impossible.

When you lack the resources of God's love, it can seem as if you and your friend were trying to pitch a ball across a wide canyon. You'll miss each other more often than you hit.

4. Take a look at how you view people. We can base our opinions of ourselves, others, and God on three models. Which fits you most closely?

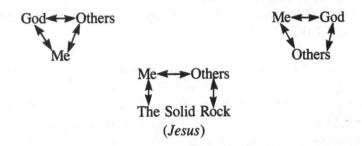

The first triangle describes the way selfish people think of everyone they contact. Only judging by their own likes and dislikes, they make themselves the basis of every choice and opinion. By founding their ideas of what is good on themselves, they miss out on many of the benefits God and other people could offer them.

In the second triangle we see the way people pleasers view the world. No matter what the issue, they base their opinions on "what will other people think?" Even though a person may have much to offer, he will never give it to the world as long as he continually defers to everyone else's ideas. People pleasers will never stand up for Jesus in a crowd, because "other people" might not agree.

If you fall in with either of these views, they will enslave you to people. You stand on the person point, and because people are weak, they will always fail you.

The view with God as its base encourages real communication and friendship. It works. With God as your foundation, you can have a true opinion of yourself. You can see when your opinion has value and when you need to defer to others.

5. Stop comparing yourself with others. Don't look at the TV and imagine that everyone has such a perfect family life. When you look at the other teens in your school's halls, they may seem to have better friendships. Don't let these idealistic comparisons make you feel blue. Chances are, you do not see the whole picture.

What reasons do you have to feel good about yourself? Look inside and see yourself the way God sees you. Search out good companions and friendships. Don't keep feeling down on yourself when you have so much to share.

6. Get involved. If you wait for others to ask you to join the group or go somewhere, they may never know you are interested. Ask if you can come. Take part in something you've always wanted to try. Bring together some people you'd like to have for friends.

Don't sit around looking at the yearbook, feeling sorry for yourself, or walk down the halls, wishing you had a friend. Find someone who needs one.

As you do these things, you'll probably feel a whole lot better. By becoming involved with others, you'll take your mind off your own troubles.

But if you remain blue for more than a couple of weeks, and you don't feel any better, or if a serious problem causes your depression, seek out counseling. You don't have to feel this way, and help is available. Don't hide your head in a cloud when there's all that sun out there!

I can't control my anger. At home and at school I always blow my top and do things I regret. How can I overcome this fault?

From time to time anger will get the best of us all, if we don't have a plan to avoid it. Uncontrolled anger can lead to the loss of a job, friends, or family, or to abuse, rape, and even murder. So I'm glad you feel concerned about this.

First, look at what caused your anger. Are you hurt because your friend could not go to a party with you? Or did a storm ruin your plans for a trip to the beach? Some things are part of life, and you can't change them or let them control your emotions.

Let's look at five causes of anger:

1. Hurts. When someone ignores you, calls you a name, or deeply scars you emotionally, you may respond in anger. But giving in to the emotion doesn't solve your problem—it only makes it eat away inside you. Don't let another person's anger control you this way.

2. Disappointment. When you can't do something you'd planned on, you can feel frustration, which may turn into anger. What frustrates or disappoints you? Is something too challenging for you? Are you trying something you lack skills for? If so, reroute yourself. Get away from the things that cause the anger by returning to the level of your ability. If it means starting over, do so.

3. Unrealistic expectations. Quite often I become angry with my kids when they are late again, tip over a glass of milk, or act their ages. I have to remember they are only children, and this is how they learn. Identify unrealistic expectations that make you mad, and learn to overcome them. Plan ahead of time to set practical goals in the areas that touch off your emotion.

4. Pestering. Does someone bug or pester you? Maybe your little sister follows you around, looking for attention, or someone in a class always tries to talk to you. If that makes you angry, think about the fact that people stay around us because they like us—even though it may get on our nerves. Take it as a compliment, go down to that person's level, and help her.

5. An out-and-out threat. If a bully puts his fist in your face and calls you names, you are likely to get angry. That might be a *good* time to feel that way. If he's bigger than you are, you may have to run. If not, do something about it. But when it's all over, remember to forgive the offender, because otherwise your anger will master you. Control your anger, instead of allowing it to control you.

Once you know *why* you feel anger, take these steps to handle it:

1. Realize you have a problem. Be honest with yourself. If it gets the best of you, admit it. Don't continue to try to handle it the way you have been, and don't try to handle it alone. Ask God to be your helper and strength. Ask an adult who has learned to overcome anger to give you some suggestions.

2. Identify the situations that make you angry. What people, places, or things contribute to it? What thoughts go through your mind that fuel the emotion? Put down on paper what causes your anger, identifying both the cause and the feeling.

3. Set up a plan to handle your anger wisely. Once you know what causes it, come up with two or three cool-down steps. If you take the time and effort to write something down, you will know how to handle the situation. Put these steps on the dashboard of your car, on your bedstand, and inside your notebook or Bible, if anger is a big problem for you. Read them often and let them seep into your mind.

Not all angry feelings cause harm. Sometimes you can make them work for your good. For example, if you feel angry at someone or something and go out and run the fastest race you've ever run, you have taken out your anger wisely and won an award. But taking your anger out on your bedroom wall, your little brother, or your mother will mean you'll have to pay the price. Whether or not you use anger constructively is up to you. Anger can make you bitter or better. You can learn to point the finger at others, encourage yourself to have high blood pressure, and cry every time it happens, or you can take positive action.

Accept the fact that everyone has frustrating things happen to them. You won't get away from days like that, but you can overcome the emotion.

Here are some constructive ways to handle anger.

Make a joke out of it. Find something funny in the person who just called you a name or accidentally ripped your paper. Learn to laugh—kindly—at the difficult situations, and you will be one of the few people in the world who is happy and feels joy, even in a downbeat situation.

Get involved. Go jogging; play raquetball or tennis. Do something to work off your anger. The energy you use up will wipe out most of your anger.

Take a nap. If you feel overstressed, you may need more rest. A long nap will relax you and wash away many of those negative feelings.

Get creative. Have a hobby. Put your mind on something that will distract you from your problem. I just started stunt-kite flying. When I put that kite in the air, I forget everything else for a while. It's hard to be angry and active at the same time.

Take a break from the situation. Sometimes, when you feel angry, you want to strike back at the person or thing that caused the emotion. When that happens, don't act on your feelings. Get away from what bothers you—take a walk, spend some time alone, or just do something else. Spend time with God and work out the trouble before you confront another person. By holding off, you can gain control of your emotions and give yourself a chance to heal broken relationships.

I feel depressed most of the time. Emptiness fills me inside, and I have no energy. I want to feel good about my life. Please help.

You need to begin by trying to figure out why you feel this way. Is it caused by a single event you can do something about? (Did your boyfriend drop you, so you sit at home alone most of the day) Or is it something more long-term and serious? (Your father abused you).

Take some steps to help yourself.

1. Can you do something about your problem? Maybe you feel depressed because you've put on some weight. Decide what action to take. If it's only a few pounds, start eating sensibly. If you need a doctor's help, seek it. Make certain you exercise enough each day. Get with a group who can help you lose weight.

Did a friend tell you he never wants to see you again? Turn to the best friend you can have—Jesus. He has hope for you, a bright future, and answers for every trouble you will face.

2. Talk to someone you can trust. If you have a serious problem, like a family crisis that does not go away, or if the depression lasts, seek professional help. If you don't know how to find a counselor, seek out anyone who loves kids and has a caring heart: your school counselor, your parents, or a trusted aunt or uncle. Find out why the emptiness inside you does not go away. Talking will help. If you seek a professional counselor, a few visits may relieve 80 to 90 percent of the hurt. Just knowing you have somewhere to turn can give you hope.

3. Get involved with people who need you. Being around people who need you or have it worse than you do can pump you up. Help out at a day-care center. Go to the hospital and visit the elderly, or become a counselor at a camp for children with cancer. Helping others can help you.

4. Make yourself stretch mentally and grow emotionally. Start the hobby you've dreamed of but never spent time on. Enroll in a new class. Offer to do extra work at school. Do anything that will build up your confidence. Stretch and grow, and you will feel good about yourself.

5. Don't watch too much TV. Limit the time you spend watching television. Also ban all soap operas from your schedule—they continually show the lives of troubled people who have no morals. In those shows depression, deceit, and drugs look normal.

6. Stay busy. If you sit around and think about your problems, they will begin to seem larger than life. Instead join an exercise or tennis club. Become part of a sports league in which you must play or exercise on a regular basis. By joining a group, you will force yourself to go regularly.

7. Read inspirational, uplifting, hopeful material at bedtime and first thing in the morning. You will put hope, excitement, and beauty in your heart and mind, and that will push out the bad, depressing thoughts. Read ten minutes of Psalms or Proverbs. Go to a local Christian bookstore and ask for books that will help you grow spiritually and mentally.

Stay away from New Age materials and run from anything that has to do with the occult, Satanism, crystals, and eastern religions. If you read fiction, beware of books that have these underlying themes (especially some science fiction). Satan runs anything occult, and he would be pleased to get you depressed enough to take your own life.

8. Don't talk with everyday people about your problems. Seek out a counselor or one special adult, but don't ask everyone's opinion. If you do, in a little while you won't know what to think, because everyone will give you a different idea. Many people's negative advice will only bring you down.

9. Use positive words. Make *beautiful, caring, love, honesty,* and *integrity* part of your vocabulary. Don't be *bummed out, lousy,* or think, *No one cares.*

Have a cheerful word for everyone you meet. When someone asks, "How are you doing?" say, "Better and better." If she says, "Have you been sick?" tell her, "You don't have to be sick to get better and better."

10. Write a blessed list. Put twenty things God has blessed you with down on paper. Think of things you haven't earned, paid for, or worked for (start with your eyesight, hearing, the abilities to walk, talk, and think).

11. Write a success list. What have you worked for and earned? If you put forth energy and got results, add it to this list. (I learned to read, write, ride a bike, play baseball, knit a sweater, save money. . . .)

12. Forgive others and be forgiven yourself. If you have to make up with a friend, do it. Go to that person and ask forgiveness for the hurt you caused. Go to God and accept His forgiveness. He has already sent His Son, Jesus, to die for all (yes, *all*) the sins of the world, including yours.

Forgive yourself for not being perfect; no one else is, either.

13. Avoid pornography. Stay away from any movie, magazine, video, TV show, or book that puts people down. Pornography degrades everyone. Satan uses it as one of his greatest tools to destroy or depress people.

14. Avoid things that will give you a "short high." Alcohol and drugs make you feel good for a while, but in the end they can only depress you. Sex outside of marriage may look good, until you experience the guilt and self-worth damage and run the risk of pregnancy or AIDS. God says it's wrong because He does not want you hurt this way. Too much sugar will raise you high and crash you on the pavement. It also makes you susceptible to sickness. Avoid caffeine, which wires and expires you.

Get help—you are worth it. Get someone to talk to. Get active, get close to God, and get on with your life. Become involved in today—don't dwell on yesterday or tomorrow.

My friend has been dieting for a long time. Something seems wrong—she's just not herself. I wonder if she is anorexic, but I don't know much about it. How can I help?

Anyone who has anorexia needs a friend like you, who cares and wants to help. This very dangerous disease occurs largely in teenagers, and about 90 percent of the time an anorexic is female.

If your friend is anorexic, she doesn't feel very good about herself. She has a strong drive to be perfect and accepted, but because she doesn't feel good enough, she tries to become popular by avoiding eating. Her low self-image actually causes her to starve herself.

In a related disease, bulimia, girls will overeat compulsively and then force themselves to vomit. Their weight may remain normal, but they endanger their health all the same.

Anorexics and bulimics open their bodies to serious illnesses and all kinds of long-lasting problems. The sooner your friend finds help, the better.

When I counsel with anorexic girls, I notice that society has won them over. They look at the glamour ads, the commercials, the bathing suits and beauty queens. They wholeheartedly buy into the idea that no one will love them if they are not pencil thin.

Once I asked some of these girls, "Do you believe in God?"

"Yes," they answered.

"Do you believe in Jesus?"

"Yes." All three told me they had asked Him into their hearts.

"Does that mean He is your Lord?"

"Yes."

"No, it doesn't." I told them. "Because if He were your Lord, He would mean more to you than anything in the world. Obviously popularity means more to you than Jesus, or you would not do this to yourself, to make yourself more popular."

Anorexics have strong wills. Otherwise they wouldn't think they had to make themselves perfect. God knows they're not perfect, but He made them with incredible detail. If they thought about how He made their bodies to work in a way that far surpasses the finest computer, they would know that He loves them and has made them special. If they could really grab ahold of that, they wouldn't have to starve themselves to look pretty.

I asked some boys who were in the same room, "Do you think they look glamorous or pretty?"

"No, they are too skinny. They look sickening," the boys replied.

"Do you wish they had more weight?"

"Absolutely."

Even though the girls were doing it all to look better, they actually made themselves less attractive. Yet they *still* had the idea they were too fat.

Perhaps your friend heard someone say she needed to lose weight. She did lose it, but then she turned the habit into a cycle.

She wanted to lose more . . . and more . . . until she couldn't stop.

Help your friend go to a counselor or her doctor. She will probably need a combination of medical help and counseling. Her whole family may need guidance, to change this. She and her parents must understand that anorexia could become a life-threatening problem, if they leave it alone.

Don't delay. Make certain your friend takes steps to solve her problems. It's worth her whole life.

3

Is There a Relationship Between Dating, Sex, and the Rest of Life?

Why should my parents have the right to tell me how long to stay out on dates? Everyone else stays out longer than I do, and it just isn't fair. How can I change their minds?

Your parents have the right to tell you how long to stay out on dates. You live in their house, and they are responsible for you. In most cases—unless some sort of abuse exists in your family—no one has spent more energy, heartache, or effort on raising you than your mom and dad. No one loves you more than they do—except God.

While you obey your parents, you have a special protection

over you. That's right—God gives this protection if you remain under your parents' love and obey and honor them. It's almost as if raindrops were trying to hit you from above, but your parents' protection covers you like a roof. Once you move out of that protection by disobeying them or lying to them, the lightning can strike. Yes, when you obey your parents, you may be susceptible to the harms of this world, but not as greatly as when you step out from their protection.

I think the real question here is Why do you want to change your parents' minds? You seem to rebel at coming in on time. Why are you interested in doing things your way? Isn't the idea of doing the right thing important to you?

Recently I saw a TV show about teens who abused their parents. One boy shared that the drugs he used kept him from realizing how much he frightened and hurt his mother. While he was on drugs, he rebelled, hating authority and only wanting to do his own thing. Today he feels ashamed but glad that he hit rock bottom, so he could get the treatment he needed and realize how much drugs and their culture influenced him.

You may not take things as far as he did, but your culture, too, can affect you. So what if others stay out later than you do? Supposedly "everyone" also drinks and uses drugs. Does that mean you have to? Very few people wear their seat belts, but what about you? Almost anybody in your school can use the greatest profanity known to man—what about you? People all over the world lie, must you?

Does the fact that others do it mean it's good for you? No! In a few years, you probably won't even know the people who influence you now. Just three years after you graduate, you probably won't have contact with them. Will you let them make you do things today you'll regret for a lifetime?

Imagine that you just got a phone call. A policeman explained that your parents were killed in an auto accident. Would you wish they were there to set that curfew time? Go talk with kids whose parents never gave them a curfew. Ask what total freedom feels like. Those teens would give anything to have parents who loved and cared enough to set limits for them.

Don't let the world influence the way you live more than the people whom you love the most. Get on your knees and thank God for your parents. Recognize that they love you, and that is why they can spot your bad friends or tell that you lied. In the short run, you might get away with wrongdoing, but in the end, you will pay. Remain in your parents' will, and you won't have that pain.

How do you act on a date so the guy will ask you out again?

When you date, don't do it to impress someone else, to show off, or for any other negative reason. Go out because you want to get to know this person and because you accept him as he is.

These nine guidelines will help you in your dating:

1. Be yourself. Don't pretend to be your best friend or the most popular girl in the school. Don't act the way you think your date would want you to act.

I watched *Cinderella* with my children. To find out who was for real, the prince tested several girls he danced with. "Isn't the sun shining brightly?" he asked that night. All the girls agreed with him. When he told them the moon was purple, they went along with it. As he danced, he started to trip over his own feet, and soon everyone else copied him. Only Cinderella asked, "Why are you acting this way? Are you trying to get people to laugh at you?" He chose her because she acted honestly.

Don't pretend you are anything you aren't—be yourself.

2. Don't get physically involved. People in school and society may tell you that you have a better chance of keeping your boyfriend if you become involved physically, but just the opposite is true. The moment you become involved physically, your boyfriend will want more and more. You will never communicate the way you did before, and your whole relationship will become physical.

Remember, as soon as a girl has sex with a guy, she is no longer a challenge. He has used and conquered her; usually he becomes history in a short time.

3. Don't put yourself in situations where you have to compromise. If you do, you will regret your actions. It's not enough to say no to sex. Don't get near parties where drugs are available or go to a place where you know there will be no chaperones. Use your mind—not just your heart and hormones—when you date.

4. Treat your date with respect. If you do, he is more likely to treat *you* with respect. If he doesn't treat you well, do you really want to see him often?

5. Demand the very best for yourself. Keep this relationship aboveboard, and remember that *you* are worth waiting for. Chances are very good that you will not marry this person, so don't do something that will cause you lifelong regret.

6. Lighten up and have fun. Don't try to be perfect or wait for the perfect date before you enjoy yourself. Stressing yourself out like that will not make either of you happy. Just because you stick to your principles doesn't mean you have to be a deadhead. Laugh often and be full of joy.

7. Ask your date questions about himself. This will show you are interested in *him*. Focus on him, and he will feel important. Don't try to top his story with a better one. Never interrupt. Be a great listener and encourager. These guidelines will help you keep your date and will teach you a lifetime full of good human-relation rules. (The same guidelines will help a guy keep his date.)

8. Plan fun, interesting dates. Get away from the ordinary and dull. Move toward new things; try something you've always wanted to do; go to new places. Movies and dances never encourage communication. Get creative!

9. Keep conversation alive. Don't force the other person, so you have to ''pull teeth'' to get him to open up. Remain cheerful and don't let little things get you down. Keep those communication lines open.

Some of my friends say that if you believe in Jesus you shouldn't date a non-Christian, but I've been seeing this really terrific guy who doesn't know the Lord. None of the Christian guys I know want to date me, so what's wrong with dating him?

It's not always easy to decide whom you should date, especially when you hear the voices of so many people, and they all seem to have a different set of rules for dating.

I don't want to burden you with a lot of rules and regulations, but think about these things:

1. There may be nothing wrong, but be careful! Maybe you want to reach this guy for Jesus. Like the Lord, you want to go to sinners and share His love with them. But Jesus never became best friends or so emotionally involved with unbelievers that He compromised and went their way. Don't open yourself to a lifestyle that does not honor God.

The problem with dating a terrific guy is that your emotions and heart can become too involved for you to let go. Many people start out dating a non-Christian, hoping to lead him to the Lord. Instead the two fall in love, get married, and year after year the Christian prays for that closest companion to find the Lord. The haunting thought that her spouse might spend eternity in hell consumes and worries her.

2. Make yourself available to Christian guys. If you separate yourself from Christians by spending all your time with unbelievers, you can't be available to guys who know the Lord. As long as they know you're dating someone, they probably won't feel they can ask you out. Don't get hung up on a non-Christian and bypass all the believers.

3. Realize your major difference. A Christian and non-Christian can share many similar interests, but one difference remains: If your boyfriend rejects Jesus, he also rejects what you stand for.

Your heart should ache for his spiritual condition, enough that you want to show him God's love and to confront him with the need to make a decision for Christ, but if he rejects Jesus, don't date him.

You can remain friends, doing things in groups, but don't get involved. Once a guy has you wrapped around his finger, head over heels in love with him, he will see no reason to accept Jesus.

How can I tell if I'm in love?

Remember when you were in elementary school, and boys didn't think girls existed, while girls wouldn't touch a boy? Then one day you reached puberty, your eyes popped out, and you noticed the opposite sex. Everything had changed!

Now when you meet a special someone you wonder, *Is* this *the one?* When you ask advice, someone tells you, "You'll know when you're in love. Don't worry about it." That friend might mean well, but it's not necessarily true. Often teens mistake infatuation, puppy love, or excitement over the opposite sex for real love.

It's no wonder teens feel confused. Fifty years ago, girls entered puberty at fifteen years old; today they do at twelve. Boys once entered puberty at sixteen; today they do at thirteen. In addition, the media and America's attitude preach, "If it feels good, do it," so teens feel ready to rush into love. Don't let that bounce you into a substitute for love.

When you meet that someone, ask yourself:

1. Am I ready to date? It's wise to wait until you are sixteen, because you'll need maturity to know when you're dating wisely. At first, go out in groups. Make certain you can totally respect your date and the other people in the group. You'll want to be sure you never take advantage of someone else and that he or she will not take advantage of you. "Love" is a poor reason to give up your virginity, and it's an even worse reason to get married.

2. What are my reasons for dating? Have you got the right motives and right direction when you are around people of the opposite sex? Do you seek pleasure at all costs—even if that means having sex before marriage and justifying it by claiming you're "in love"? Are you willing to risk a sexually transmitted disease, because love "entitles" you to go all the way? Are you willing to lose your friendships with your parents and God? Do you want to become a liar and a deceiver in order to experience that pleasurable feeling?

Wrong motives can leave you haunted by visions of people of whom you have taken advantage or who have taken advantage of you.

3. Am I looking toward the future? You will probably date many people before you marry. You have the rest of your life before you. Someday be able to tell your children, "I believe I was worth waiting for. Even though I lived through a time of sexual revolution, I waited until my partner and I were bonded in holy matrimony to have sex. We have built our love on the foundations of truth, honesty, and integrity."

Are you really in love? It's great to have strong feelings for a member of the opposite sex, but don't let those emotions engulf you. A lifetime of regret is simply not worth it.

My boyfriend claims the Bible doesn't really say we can't have sex before marriage, and anyway, he doesn't even want to go all the way. What should I say to him?

Since you asked this question, I think you know that you need to say no, even if it's hard. Don't worry! You have good reasons for your answer.

1. Show your boyfriend what the Bible says. Read Genesis 2:24 together: "For this reason a man will leave his father and mother and will be united to his wife, and they will become one flesh." That's God's plan for sex: one man, one woman, within marriage.

Follow this up with Hebrews 13:4 (*italics added*): "Marriage should be honored by all, and the marriage bed kept pure, for God will judge the adulterer and *all the sexually immoral.*"

2. Remember, the Bible doesn't spell out everything. Though the Scriptures don't tell you what to do on a date, they do show you the kind of life God wants you to cultivate. From that you can make a decision. The next time you have to choose, remember this ditty: "If the answer isn't black or white, will it lead to wrong or right?" You know that God wants the marriage bed to be kept pure. Will what you are doing put that in danger?

3. Don't compromise. If you cheated on a test for the first eight questions, but resisted on the last two, you still went too far. As a result, you'll think less of yourself and move closer to becoming a full-time cheater. Practice makes permanent! It's the same with sex.

4. He won't be satisfied until he can go all the way. Maybe he won't do it the first time, but you're starting a bad habit that will keep on escalating. When he stops thinking with his head and turns on his hormones, you are both in trouble.

5. Boys and girls are different. I know you know about the major physical differences, but when it comes to motives, they're different, too. Girls will give sex to get love; guys give love (and every line in the world) to get sex.

6. Pain and heartache will follow. When he leaves because you are no longer a challenge—he has conquered you—you will feel broken apart. Pain goes deep into the heart and remains there, so don't give it a chance to enter.

7. You'll both lose respect. When the challenge is gone, his respect will be, too. Once you give in, you'll feel the sting of loss of self-respect. Keep your self-esteem by doing the right thing.

8. You deserve better than this. Set your standards high, because you are worth it. Don't budge even a little, or you'll build up high hopes and envision giving in. By never lowering your standards, you can remain safe.

9. Make your goals clear. Before every date, have it well understood that you are saving yourself for marriage, period! Don't go anywhere until you and your boyfriend pray for God's safety and protection. When you do this, you'll be surprised at the improvement you'll see in his actions!

> **My boyfriend says either we have sex, or it's over. I know it would be wrong to have sex with him, but I don't want to lose him. He's all I have. What can I do?**

You have to change what you have—or maybe take a new look at what you *think* you have. If your boyfriend remains everything to you, you'll act out of desperation—having sex with him and regretting it for a lifetime.

In this situation, you have three choices:

- You can have sex now and feel sorry later. If you do give in to him, chances are things won't work out, and you'll have a broken heart to show for your pains. The more you become involved with him, the greater the risk of hurt.
- You can have sex now and rush into marriage. Even if you do marry, you will not have a well-rounded relationship, but

one headed for disaster. Because you're starting from a weak base, I can almost guarantee that the marriage will never work out.

• You can say no now. Maybe he will leave you, and for a while it *will* hurt, but you will have invested in your future. When you do marry, you will be able to do so with pride.

Taking the step of refusing him may seem hard at first—it *is* a tough decision. But make the right choice because you know it's right, not because it won't hurt. Don't stop there, either.

1. Look at the other things in your life. You say he's all you have. But have you looked at the other things in your life that you've put on the back burner? How about your family, friends (some of whom you may not have seen in a while), and God?

Make pleasing God your first priority, and follow it with getting close to family and friends. Start a new hobby. Write to missionaries; start a Bible study, or join one that's going on. Soon you'll have a lot more than you thought.

2. Stand by your convictions. Since you know it's wrong, don't do it. If your boyfriend comes back later and tries to convince you to change your mind, stand firm. Better to lose him than give in, washing away your integrity, virginity, and self-worth.

3. Tell him why you're saying no. Say, "I'm worth waiting for. If you really loved me, you wouldn't want to compromise my morals. If you *do* love me enough to marry me someday, we will experience sex together for the first time on our honeymoon."

Don't be swept away into marriage because he wants sex. Don't let a desire for pleasure on your honeymoon lead you to a quick decision that could make you miserable your whole life.

Before you marry, be certain this is a lifetime commitment—one you can make with someone who shares your interests and values.

4. Help him with his beliefs and character qualities. Your boyfriend should know what he stands for and what he stands against. If you have to provide moral backbone for both of you, the future will become pretty grim. Who's the leader—you or him?

5. Share Jesus with him. If you know Jesus, and he doesn't, you live in two different worlds. Your priorities are completely different from his. That's why God doesn't want Christians dating non-Christians. He doesn't want you married to someone with whom you have nothing in common. Unless he knows Jesus, your relationship has a dead end.

Right now you have a choice to make. What you decide can make you strong or harm your life. Let Jesus help you make the right one!

My boyfriend uses drugs and even sells them sometimes. Though I love him, I don't like what he's doing. How can I respond?

Your boyfriend is really the one who has to make the choice, not you. He must decide between drugs and you: He can use the drugs or build a friendship and relationship with you.

If he chooses to use drugs, you really have no logical choice except to say, "So long, Charlie." If you choose to stay with him while he uses drugs (or alcohol):

1. You could have legal problems. You may get arrested and convicted if he is with you, gets caught, and has the drugs with him. Whether or not you take them, you have been part of breaking the law.

2. You could lose your reputation. Even if you never take the drugs, you will have the reputation of a drug user. People will judge you by the company you keep, and you can't blame them— they see you with the wrong crowd.

3. You will set yourself up for a gigantic heartache. If he can't stop now, he may still be hooked later on, when he makes so much money that he won't be able to stop. By that time you may be hopelessly in love. Ask the survivors of such drug-riddled love affairs how much pain they have experienced—pain they could have avoided.

4. You could face serious troubles. You could become hooked on drugs and have an overdose, or get AIDS, or give birth to a brain-damaged child. *Now* is the time to avoid all this trouble.

5. You could try to run away. If things go badly at home, you could run away and become a street kid. Because you could not get a job, you'd probably have to turn to prostitution for survival.

There are plenty of good reasons for not staying with him, but not many to remain. If you break up, you will feel brokenhearted for a while, but you can live through that. Once you have ended this relationship, you can get on with your life, with healthy relationships, and your friendships with your parents and God.

The lady at Planned Parenthood told my boyfriend and I to use protection, since we were already having sex regularly. After hearing your speech at my school, I don't know if this protection is good enough. Help!

Any time a health official gives a teenager a condom, I ask that teen to respond, "Would you use the same protection if you were having sex tonight with a person you knew had AIDS?" If the official answers honestly, he or she will say, "No." Studies show that condoms fail about 17 percent of the time. Recently, in Florida, over 50,000 boxes had to be recalled, because the condoms had two holes in them.

You cannot have safe sex outside of a marriage in which both people have been totally faithful to each other and have abstained from sex prior to marriage. No "good enough" protection from premarital sex exists. What will protect you from your boyfriend's leaving you? What can keep you from the heartache, pain, and shame? What will protect you when your self-worth hits rock bottom? You have been used and conquered, and you have given up your virginity; nothing guards against the hurt that comes with that knowledge. What effective barrier lies between you and the possibility of AIDS or herpes? A condom can never be enough. Sex lasts for a moment, but herpes sticks with you for a lifetime.

Planned Parenthood won't tell you all those truths, because it is in the business of reproduction prevention and abortion. As long as it stays in that business, it gets money from the government. If all teens abstained from sex, or if Planned Parenthood taught every pregnant girl to give her baby up for adoption, it would probably go out of business.

Do the people at Planned Parenthood want the best for you; do they want something from you; or do they want the profit they can get through you? Evaluate the people who give you advice. Do they truly have your best interests at heart?

If you and your boyfriend continue to have sex, what are the possible long-term results? Are they worth it? I don't think so.

Plenty of sex therapists and experts tell us we can have "safe sex." You don't seem to agree with them. Why?

Why do the people who proclaim safe sex tell you you can have premarital sex with impunity? Look at their ideas and life-styles to understand where their point of view comes from.

1. What do they base their knowledge on? The experts who say sex outside marriage is okay base it on their own wisdom or the wisdom of other "experts" who agree with them. They will tell you premarital sex is fun, that you have these "natural" urges you simply can't control, and that it's okay as long as "no one gets hurt."

Do these people talk to the hurting teens who have lost their self-esteem? Do they hear the tears in the voice of the girl who has lost her virginity, only to have a boyfriend move on to another girl? Can they see the children born to teens for whom "safe sex" failed?

Just because an expert tells you sex is okay doesn't make it right for you or free of consequences.

2. Health officials get paid to preach safe sex. Federal funds foot the bill for many abortions, condoms, and clinics. If the people who worked in the clinics told teens to do things God's way, first they'd be labeled *religious,* then they'd talk themselves out of a job.

While these people see things in terms of their own careers and desire to tell people to do what feels good, they can't seem to understand the hurt this life-style causes in countless lives.

What do safe-sex supporters believe about sex? Take a look.

1. Adultery is okay. As long as "no one knows," "no one is hurt," or the relationship is "meaningful," to them, sex outside marriage is fine. What of the wife who discovers that her husband has had an affair? What of the sense of failure that overwhelms a husband who learns his wife became pregnant by another man and had an abortion? Broken homes and hearts mean little to these "experts."

2. There is nothing wrong with exploiting women and children through pornography. These people seem not to care that a large percentage of pornography ends up before the eyes of young, impressionable children. They must avoid reading the statistics that connect rape with pornography. Meanwhile the experts speak out for a woman's "rights," but what woman wants the "right" to be raped?

3. Homosexuality is an acceptable "alternative life-style." Though AIDS has devastated the homosexual community and there is much pain in the life of the homosexual, the "experts" encourage people to believe it's a good thing. They can tell homosexuals how to have "safe sex," but they cannot guarantee that a condom will always prevent AIDS; neither can they guarantee that anyone who becomes involved in homosexuality will be happier.

4. One-night stands are okay. They believe that a man who takes a woman to dinner deserves to receive sex in payment. Where are they when someone has to heal the damage a one-night-stand life-style inflicts on both partners?

5. People can't say no to sexual urges. They encourage teens to have sex because they believe no one can say no. And of course as long as you don't want to say no, you won't.

Let's look at some of the truths they have left out of their argument:

1. Outside marriage, there is no safe sex. Look at the physical and emotional facts.

> • Sex outside marriage leaves you with a feeling of being used. Long after your partner of the moment is gone, that feeling will remain.
> • Condoms fail up to 17% of the time.
> • The Pill cannot give you full protection. Even women who take the Pill sometimes get pregnant.
> • AIDS is 100% deadly. This is one disease you cannot recover from—and you can never be sure you will not catch it, unless you and your partner keep sex within marriage only.

2. Teens *can* say no to sex. You can make decisions about sex, based on your knowledge of what is right and wrong. Learn what God says is right and stick to it. Don't abandon your beliefs because someone turns up the pressure on you.

You are not an alley cat. There's more to you than your body, and you can control what your body does.

God created you. He knows what it's like to face the pressure, and He has provided you with a way out. He loved you enough to send His Son to die for you on the cross. Jesus will forgive your sins, if you totally trust Him for your salvation. He can also give you the strength to withstand the temptation to fall in with the "experts" or give in to the pressures of a date.

3. You never have to "pay" for a date. The idea that a girl owes a guy sex because he took her out is hogwash. Don't fall for that kind of lie. The girl who gives in to a guy's pressure and the guy who gives in to temptation will have to live with the pain of knowing they have failed. Don't start yourself on a bad cycle; or if you have failed already, turn to God for forgiveness. Make Him the center of your dating, and you need not fail again.

4. God knows and cares about your sex life. The Lord has made it perfectly clear that sex before or outside marriage is wrong and harmful. He calls it sin. Because He knows it will only hurt you, He warns you away from it.

The experts who tell you "no one will ever know" do not believe in God or do not think He cares. They do not consider the fact that they will someday answer to Him for their acts. No matter what you do, God knows about it, and He cares enough for you to want only the best in your life.

I hope you have *really* safe sex—the kind God talks about. If you do, you will have the blessing of knowing you have lived to His standard; you will never have to worry about AIDS or venereal disease; and you can have a marriage that is not harmed by the memories of failures and sin. Saying no today will make you happy now and in the future.

Why should teens who have already lost their virginity wait until marriage to have sex again? What harm could come from it?

Losing your virginity may be a one-time thing, but it is not the only thing. God does not say about you, "Oh, she lost her virginity, so nothing else she does matters." He never gives up on you, so don't give up on yourself.

By continuing to have sex, you will run risks:

1. Physically. Every time you have sex, you increase your chances of getting pregnant and picking up a sexually transmitted disease. You may have lost your virginity, but do you need to lose your future—or your life?

2. Emotionally. The more you have sex, the more you will feel like an object. You will lose the knowledge that you are a unique, lovable person. Until you stop, your self-worth will go further and further down the drain.

If you are having sex to feel accepted and important, it will never work. The emotional impact can only be negative, in the long run.

3. Mentally. You will fill your memory with more and more sex partners. When you marry, you will compare your spouse to these men. Many marriages end because one spouse cannot live up to the other's memory of previous sexual experiences.

4. Spiritually. As you have premarital sex, you build up guilt. Each time you have sex you draw farther away from God, and it's harder and harder to return to His standard. In the end, you may turn from Him so often that your heart becomes hardened to Him.

If you do decide never again to have sex outside of marriage, you can expect good things to happen:

1. You will enhance your self-worth and esteem. Saying, ''I goofed up, but I'm not going to anymore. I've learned my lesson, accepted God's forgiveness, and now I'm moving forward in my life,'' means you can have respect for yourself.

2. You will set a good pattern in your life. In this, and other things, you need to know how to (a) recognize your mistakes, (b) stop making them, and (c) have the courage not to start again. Carry over such decision-making ability to each part of your life.

3. You will remove the cause of much guilt. Premarital sex is a main cause of guilt between teens and parents and teens and God. By making this decision, you will restore your inner health and rebuild shattered roadways between you and the people you care about. It's never too late to do right.

4. You can focus on God's forgiveness. You can become a virgin again in His eyes. Be pure in His eyes, and you'll fall in love with the person you see in your mirror each day. God has enough love, grace, and kindness to fill your heart with the self-respect you need.

Once you become clean and spotless in God's sight, by seeking His forgiveness and living for Jesus, you become a virgin again in His sight! And if you have ever lost your virginity through force, as in the case of sexual abuse or rape, you have *always* remained a virgin in God's eyes.

> **I'm pregnant, alone, and scared. My parents would kill me, if I told them. It's as if all the problems in the world are fighting inside me, and I don't have any answers. I can't handle this alone—write back fast!**

Don't handle this alone.

I know it seems as if your parents would kill you if they found out, and maybe they will blow up or get hysterical, but they will not kill you. I have yet to hear of a single case in which a parent killed a pregnant daughter. However, I have heard of many cases in which the daughter wishes she *had* gone to her parents. Often dads and daughters—as well as moms and daughters—have become much closer because they lived through such a difficult situation. They have even become best of friends.

If your daughter had this happen, wouldn't you want her to come to you? How would you feel, if you knew you had raised her for all those years, and one day, because of a pleasurable act, she got pregnant and then went for an abortion that you only heard about secondhand? Wouldn't you want to be there, so you could talk to her and offer help? Wouldn't you want the chance to share with her that God had given the baby life, and you can't take that away by abortion, just because it might seem like an awkward interference?

Go to your parents. Tell them how you feel; share the hurt, the pain, and the confusion inside you. Let them be part of this decision.

Look into adoption. Thousands of couples—like my wife, Holly, and I—cannot have children. For years we tried to have our own. We went through test after test. We begged, prayed, and waited for five years on the first adoption list, before we got Emily. Since then we have found out that Emily's mother became a Christian, and someday, when Emily is old enough, we want her to see her birth mother. We cannot wait for her to find the woman who loved her enough, through that painful, confusing time, to give her life. Though Emily may never link up with her down here, she knows her biological mother will spend eternity with her in heaven. Her mother knows Emily lives in a home with two loving parents who consider God first and foremost, know right from wrong, and want to raise her to be a God-loving and God-respecting Christian girl.

When we adopted the twins, we met their mother and saw the love she had for them. In letter after letter, she described to her babies why she didn't want them to live in anything but the best situation. Alone, she could not do that, so she gave them up for adoption. I saw her say good-bye to the twins and come back to give Emily a big hug, tears filling her eyes. After she left the building, she came back to give a gift to Emily, so she wouldn't feel left out.

I know real love because I have seen it in action in these mothers' lives. Today we would not have our children, except for the unselfish giving of these women. They provided our kids with the gifts of life, love, and time.

Go to a Christian counselor or adoption agency that will make certain you receive the proper advice. Talk to them and find out that you can choose the type of parent your child will have. Discover the facts from people who want to help you.

Pray during this tough time. God is there to help. He knows about the pain; He was abandoned Himself. The very people He came to save killed Him on the cross. He, who gave up paradise to come to earth, was ridiculed and murdered. For three days He even went to hell so we would not have to go there, if we trust in His love.

With God, your parents, and professionals who want the best for you and your baby, you can turn this into a positive thing. Make it a life-giving situation instead of a life-taking one.

In the past my dad abused me, and I hate him for it. My boyfriend and I plan to run away and get married, as soon as school is over; but how can I be sure my life won't turn out just like my parents'? Help!

Before you go *anywhere,* go for professional counseling. Abuse has left you with scars, hurts, and troubles that you cannot fix alone.

Running away will not solve your problems; it will only make things a hundred times worse. Why? Because whether or not you realize it, girls base their expectations for their husbands on what they did or didn't see in their fathers.

I'm sure you don't want to end up as an abused wife or a husband abuser. If you don't resolve the things that have happened in your family, you may end up in one of these situations. Either way the odds are heavily against your marriage working out. It will probably only last a few years—or even months.

Many people go into marriage expecting this new spouse to solve their problems. But no person can do that successfully, so from the spouse, they go on to transfer those expectations onto the children, a new home, or something else. Meanwhile, they're drowning in the sea of problems that surrounded them from the start. The time to deal with problems is *before* you marry.

If you marry without relieving the pressure from this abuse, someday it will explode. Perhaps heat will build up a little at a time, over months or years—or it may happen rapidly. Counseling can help cool things down. Then, if you still wish to marry, you and your boyfriend will have a chance.

Talk with your boyfriend and tell him that marriage has to wait. If he insists on marrying now, he, too, is hurrying things. Marriage lasts a lifetime; waiting a few more months—or even years—is not the end of the world. If neither of you can hold off, think what it could mean for the next year or so of your marriage.

I believe you know the truth in your heart. Getting help will not be easy. You will have to confront issues and deal with them a little at a time, but the gains in your future will make it all worthwhile. Fight the uphill battle now—while you are single—or you will have a husband, children, and others deeply entangled in your confusion.

4
Where Do I Go When I Need a Friend?

Why is peer pressure so powerful? How can it make teens do so many things they regret?

Not all peer pressure causes regrets. It really comes in three varieties:

1. Harmful peer pressure: This is anything that could hurt you, like the pressure from others to use drugs or stay out of school.

2. Helpful peer pressure: Some peer pressure can challenge you. It might encourage you to improve yourself by studying harder or spending more time practicing a musical instrument.

3. Ho-hum peer pressure: Some things really don't matter. For example, you may eat the same lunch your friend does or wear the same colors she likes. Chances are, these will not hurt you.

The greatest culprit often isn't peer pressure at all. Many teens give it the bad rap for their own decisions. After all, chances are slim that someone will put a gun to your head to make you smoke, drink, or avoid using your seat belt. A teen who does these things actually pressures himself because he wants acceptance. Though no one ordered him not to use the seat belt, he imagines another teen will see him snap it on and decide then and there not to be friends. Before he knows it, he's doing what "everyone else" does—even if "everyone else" is all in his head.

People pressure themselves because they want to be accepted, wanted, loved, and needed. Avoid putting so much pressure on yourself by following these guidelines:

1. Accept yourself. Look inside yourself and know you are okay just the way you are. You don't have to do anything you don't believe in just to fit in with any group.

2. Realize others accept you. Identify those who love you as you are. Make a list of people who love you for yourself, not what you will or won't do for them. These are your real friends.

3. Identify your hidden desires. Ask yourself why you want to be wanted. Do you expect a certain group to admit you to its ranks because of your money, car, looks, ability to follow the crowd, and so on? Friendships based on these are shallow. What will happen if you lose those things?

4. Seek common interests. Don't put unnecessary pressure on yourself. If you don't feel comfortable with a group, don't spend years trying to fit in with them. Get other friends. Naturally it takes time to build friendships, and when you first join a new crowd it may take a while to discover common interests, but don't stay forever with a group you can't share in.

5. Remain firm in doing right. Keep your standards. Don't compromise who or what you are just to gain a group's acceptance.

How can I be a Christian and keep from losing all my friends?

Knowing Jesus doesn't mean you can't have any friends, but it will make a difference in how you treat others and how they treat you. Now that Jesus is your Best Friend, you'll want to draw others to Him, and you'll notice the difference in your relationships.

First, avoid these things in your friendships.

1. Don't act better than others. God offered you His grace and love, and you asked Jesus to be your Savior and Lord. That doesn't mean you have the right to go around with your nose up in the air. In fact, acting that way goes against everything Christ wants you to stand for: compassion, loving one another, and treating people with respect and dignity.

Unlike other diseases, conceit makes everyone sick except the person who has the illness. By deceiving yourself into thinking you're holier than anyone else or better than those who have not experienced God's forgiveness, you put everyone at a distance.

2. Don't flaunt your faith. When a Christian flaunts his beliefs, throwing them in others' faces, he makes them feel inferior. Resentment and then bitterness flow into the relationship. Flaunting your faith is much like bragging about your looks or special talents. No one wants to hear it, and it doesn't reflect the kind of humble life-style Jesus wants you to have.

Keep your friendships firm by not becoming untouchable or acting so special that no one wants to come near you.

3. Don't expect everyone to like you. Even if you didn't know Jesus, some people wouldn't be your friends. Wanting the whole world to love you is unrealistic.

As Christians, we know some people will not like us. Those who reject our Lord and Savior, Jesus Christ, will not like us any better. Has someone called you a Jesus freak, goody two-shoes, or a bore? The Bible says to expect it. When others tell you you're afraid because you won't go to a drinking party, you're in the best of company: Jesus Christ's.

Reacting with hostility will not improve the situation. Jesus commands us to turn the other cheek, love when others hate, hug when they push away, and pray for those who hurt us desperately.

When a friend turns her back on you because you read your Bible, pray before each meal, start a Bible study in your school, or care for the "undesirables," remember, Jesus said it would happen. Don't let her reaction keep you from your Christian testimony.

4. Don't lose respect by going along with the crowd. Once you become a Christian, people can see the difference. Don't try to hide it. As Jesus said in the Sermon on the Mount, ". . . A city on a hill cannot be hidden" (Matthew 5:14). If you've driven at night, far from a major city or town, you know when you come to the first city. You see a glow on the horizon, which grows brighter as you approach. Now you begin to look forward to finding a motel, where you can eat and sleep. Nothing hides that city.

It's the same with faith. If you had a passenger in the back-seat of your car, who slept as you drew near the city, he might not know what was going on: just so a few people might not pick up on your faith at first. But sooner or later, they'll figure it out, and if you've tried to hide your beliefs, no one will respect you.

By going along with the crowd, because that's the easy thing to do, you don't gain anything with God or your friends. If others know you are a Christian and see you at parties where people use drugs, your reputation will go right down the drain. No one will respect your faith.

Suppose someone tells a dirty joke in front of you. Don't laugh, just walk away. Avoid saying something like, "You're going to hell for telling dirty jokes." Later, when you are one-on-one with the joke teller, you may be able to gently challenge him, but never flaunt your faith.

By standing up for Jesus, you will gain respect. Today you might be in the minority, but when He comes back for us, we will be in the majority. Let people know *now* what faith means.

5. Don't hold onto a friendship at the cost of faith. Reach out to your friends for Christ, but don't feel surprised if your friendships begin to change. We cannot remain close to those who reject Jesus for long, and we tend to find friends who love Him.

Often I talk to teens who have friends with a deep involvement in heavy sin: Satanism, selling drugs, pornography, or some form of abuse. "Stand up for Jesus," I say. "Pray for your friends and challenge them, but don't really expect to keep that friendship. If you compromise, they will not respect you, and you'll lose the friendship anyway.''

Make that friendship count with God, but don't hang around sin for too long, or you will no longer stand firm and talk and share Jesus. Don't let anything deter you from friendship with Him.

On the positive side, you can take these steps:

1. Live the way the Bible says to. Remember how everyone walked past the man who had been mugged on the way to Jericho?—everyone except the Good Samaritan. Others walked by because they didn't want to be seen with him or feared for their lives if they helped the man on this dangerous road. But the Samaritan didn't care what people thought or who might attack him.

To keep friends and have their numbers grow, live as Christ would. Be a friend to someone who's lonely. By showing compassion, consideration, and encouragement, you will build others up, and who can resist that?

Live positively, and you'll have something most people want: a life-style with integrity. As Christians we have the past forgiven and the future secured. Therefore we should be the most positive, upbeat, excited, enthusiastic, and worry-free people the world has ever seen!

2. Love others without judgment. In the Sermon on the Mount Jesus clearly told us not to judge others. To win people to our Savior, we must love, not come down harshly on them. When you quickly judge a friend, without knowing her heart, you ruin your testimony. You may also ruin your chances of keeping friends in any circle.

3. Share your faith tactfully. Jesus told us to go to all the world and spread the Good News about Him. Why wouldn't we? It gives us such a wonderful feeling of contentment. We want to share that feeling and the knowledge that we have eternal life and forgiveness.

When you share your faith, do you cram it down your best friend's throat? Do you share lovingly, or is witnessing just another Christian chore? None of that is what God had in mind.

When we share, God expects us to do it tactfully and lovingly. When I speak in public high schools, I'm there to show people they can feel good about themselves, boost their self-esteem, and help them say no to drugs; I cannot do that if I imply they were a mistake or they evolved from slime or there is no hereafter. I'm not there for the sole purpose of sharing my faith, but I can't say there is no Supreme Being who keeps this universe intact.

I share using humor and love. When I speak to little kids, I ask, "Who made our thumbprints different?"

They yell out, "God did!"

In my parent sessions, I say, "You don't think there is prayer in schools? Obviously you've never been around at test time." I might add, "Even a hard quiz gets kids down on all fours, praying to God."

Lots of times I tell the story about the little boy who brought his New Testament to school. The other kids made fun of him, saying, "Religion is for sissies."

The little boy looked at the biggest of his accusers, and hand-ing him the Bible, said, "Here, see if you have the courage to carry this around school for just one hour!"

Don't lose your friends by being a Christian, because that's not what being a Christian means. Instead offer your friends God's free gift: eternal life.

You talk a lot about making your brother or sister a friend. How can I do that?

It's a good idea to make your brother or sister a friend, because that relationship could benefit you both for your whole lives. By getting started now, you can enjoy closeness for many years.

1. Look at things from your brother or sister's point of view. Your younger brother may just want to be part of your group. Your older sister may feel the pressures of looking for a college or finding a job. When you relate to them, take into account how each person thinks and what it's like to be that age.

2. Be considerate of your brother or sister. To make that easier, think about what it would be like to be an only child. If you think it would be fun, ask only children about the loneliness. Talk to a friend who has no brothers or sisters, to see it from another perspective. Perhaps you've taken your family for granted.

3. Don't let others keep you from this friendship. How much does peer pressure affect how you treat your family? Most teens fight with a sibling—at least some of the time—because their friends do it. Just because your friend doesn't think it's cool to be pals with his brother, does that mean you can't turn your sister into a friend? Decide for yourself.

How would you feel if your brother or sister had been killed? Would you wish you'd done something differently? Make those changes before it's too late.

Why do special cliques have to exist in our school?

It hurts to feel left out. No one likes to feel as if she were "on the outside, looking in." No guy wants to feel he could never be part of the team or liked by the best-looking girls in the class.

But believe it or not, there are some positive reasons why you have certain groups in your school.

1. Part of it is normal, healthy, and necessary. When people who share interests get together, they can form better friendships. If you hate baseball, you'd never feel comfortable on the team; people who can't stand chess don't really want to be in the chess club, and chances are they don't have many friends on the chess team, because they have different interests. It's the same way with other groups of people.

2. No one can have lots and lots of intimate friends. Building friendships takes time and effort. About the largest number of close friends you could have would be four, and at times you may only have one. But when you have four friends, you may not be as close to any of them as you'll be to that one.

Though you can know lots of people and care for them, you can't become truly close with twenty or thirty people at once. No one has the energy or time to nurture so many deep relationships.

So limiting friendships is not *all* bad, if it causes better relationships based on common interests and goals.

Groups can become negative, however, when they have the wrong attitude about their limitedness. No group should:

1. Put down other people. Not everyone shares the same interests; just because they're not in the group is no reason to label others *bad*.

2. Look out for only their own benefit. Such groups become self-destructive. Nothing lasts long when it has only its own good at heart.

3. Ridicule others because of some "lack." What makes any one group the best measure of people? No one has the right to gossip, be mean, or make fun of someone else who is less attractive or smart. No clique should make a person who is "different" pay for the rest of his life.

People may want to be part of groups that do these things, but you can do better for yourself. Set yourself a higher standard.

How do you relate to groups in your school? Ask yourself:

1. Am I a member of a clique? If so, how do the people in it influence you? How do you influence them? Are the morals they have good for you? I talk with many kids who became involved with drugs or partying because "the group was doing it." They didn't have the courage to stand up for themselves. Don't let yourself fall into that trap.

2. Am I feeling left out? Perhaps you feel as if you don't belong to the right group. Do you want to be friends with a certain clique because of their status? If so, you could spend your life searching for the "right" group. Instead of looking at the outside, you need to discover friends who show they are honest, sincere, have a sense of humor, and are easy to get along with.

3. Do I reach out to new people? Never assume you will not like someone new. She could end up being your next best friend or a lifelong pal. Give people a chance. If you were in her place, you'd want a fair opportunity.

Occasionally you will find someone who just never fits in. No matter what you do, he may remain beyond your group, but at least offer him the opportunity to become a friend. Give a person a chance, or he may remain isolated and hurt.

4. Am I avoiding the pettiness of some groups? Compassion and kindness are lost arts in today's world. You may have received unkind treatment from other people, but that doesn't mean you have to join in their naughty reindeer games.

You may never change every group in your school, but you can start with yourself and encourage your friends to develop these attitudes. Everyone in the school will never be close to you, but you'll probably have some good friends.

Ever since my friend got mad at me for something I did, I have felt a million miles away from God. Do you think there's a connection? What can I do about it?

There sure is a connection—but there's also a cure.

Whenever I get mad at my wife or a good friend, something happens inside me: My desire to say, "I'm sorry, will you forgive me?" turns completely off; and I no longer feel like praying. I don't want to be around anyone.

That's the problem with inside hurts and sins: They close off our feel-good buttons. But if you make a wrong right, like magic, your feel-good button and desire to get closer to God will both work again.

First John 4:20 says, "If anyone says, 'I love God,' yet hates [has wronged] his brother, he is a liar. For anyone who does not love his brother, whom he has seen, cannot love God, whom he has not seen."

Pull out your Bible and read Matthew 5:23, 24. Let it encourage you to go to your friend and say, "I'm sorry I hurt you; let's not let Satan break up our friendship. Please forgive me."

God's guideline for friendship is ". . . First go and be reconciled to your brother; then come. . ." (Matthew 5:24). You can't carry a grudge against your friend and stay close to your Best, Best Friend.

My best friend and I had a major fight. I apologized, but he still won't talk to me. It's been a long time. What can I do?

Trying to put a friendship back together can show your friend how important he is to you. But you may have to be patient before he sees that. Take the following steps:

1. Begin by going to your friend. Apologize for your part in the problem. If he does not accept the apology, it is no longer your problem—it's his. You cannot force him to be your friend, but you have tried to make peace between you.

2. Keep your cool. If you apologize and your friend gets angry, don't react in anger and get mad all over again. A good friendship allows for personality differences. Be a good friend.

3. Be patient. Once you have apologized, give your friend time to get over his anger. People recover from hurts at different rates. You may let things blow over easily, but your friend may hold onto anger for a while longer.

4. Think about this friendship. Ask yourself, *How important is this to me?* If you have to eat humble pie, then do it. Call your friend and be honest with him. Tell him you think this relationship is worth fighting for. People who risk nothing cannot have strong friendships. The closeness you gain can be worth the pain.

5. Talk with your friend. Ask him what *he* thinks caused the problem. Unless you get at the source, the problem will come up again. Plan for it not to happen, and chances are it won't.

I have tried to be nice to an unpopular boy in my class, but even when I sit with him in the lunchroom, the way you suggested, he rejects all my efforts to be friendly. What now?

First, ask yourself, *Why am I being friendly to him?* Did you do it so other teens will admire you and pat you on the back? Do you want to be noticed? He's sure to pick up on that. If you are not doing it for the recognition, but to help him, remember you need to keep on being tactful and pleasant. You may have to try to talk to this boy several times before he will talk back. Low self-esteem may shut his mouth. At first he'll find it hard to accept a compliment or almost never look you in the eyes, because he has been picked on, put down, and abused by others. Deep in the back of his mind, he wonders if you want something from him or if you are setting him up for some big heartache later. Much of this comes from self-preservation instinct. Keep trying for a while, and you may gain some ground.

If he continues to refuse you, though, stop. You may have to settle for being nice when you see him in the hallway, or maybe you can tell him to call if he ever wants to talk. You can pray for him and make certain you never spread rumors about him. Stand up for him when he needs it. But at some point he has the right to be left alone, if he will not become friendly.

Give it a little more time, if you've only made a few efforts to be nice. I think he will come around. Everyone needs someone like you, who is nice for the sake of being nice. Once you break down the wall, he may be happy to be friends.

My friend has a really serious problem, but she made me promise not to tell any one about it. I want to tell someone, because I can't help her. How do I know if I should break confidentiality?

If your friend has a problem of incest or abuse or if she is talking about suicide, you *must* break your promise. She needs help badly, and only if you tell will she get it. Whenever someone is deeply at risk, when she could hurt herself or others, or when someone is hurting her, you need to find help.

Remember, it is always better to have a live friend who can get mad at you than a dead, hurting, or abused friend, because you kept that problem a secret.

If at all possible, take your friend to someone in authority, to tell about the problem. If she will not go, go yourself.

When you counsel with someone, try not to promise ahead of time that you will not tell. However, if you make that promise without realizing what will be said, and the person you counsel tells you of one of the above problems, you must break the promise. You need to get help; it is said that in the long run 100 percent of the time that person will thank you. Your friend cannot thank you if she does not live through her problem.

By breaking that trust, you do not betray her; you have been the most loyal friend she could have. You have acted in her best interests, because you truly want the best for her. You willingly placed your friendship on the line because you cared so much for her.

Recently one of my friends told me he was considering suicide, but then he laughed it off as if it were a big joke. Should I take him seriously?

Absolutely! Whenever someone implies suicide, talks about it directly, or tells you how, where, and why, take it seriously. Go to someone who can help: your parents, a concerned teacher, a counselor who cares about kids, your principal, or someone else.

Time after time I have heard that a suicide victim had told friends the details of his plan to take his own life. Those friends ignored him or responded, "You'll never do it," or, "That's a stupid thing, so don't think about it." In several situations, the suicide took his life just the way he'd said he would.

Don't ignore anyone who mentions suicide. If your friend says he will do it that night, do not leave him. Call for help. If he makes you promise not to tell anyone, it does not matter. In a life-or-death case like this, you must break confidentiality. Your friend will thank you in the end. Let him share, then get help immediately. You can handle your friend's angry feelings later.

I think the girl who has the locker next to mine is being abused at home. Should I do something, or should I mind my own business?

How often do we see newspaper reports of neighbors who knew the kid next door was abused, but no one said a word, because everyone felt it wasn't his or her business? By the time a tragedy occurred, it was too late to help the child.

Abuse *is* your business; it is everyone's business. If you sense something this serious, go to an adult, not another teen. Do not start a rumor about your suspicions, in case you are wrong. Talk to your counselor, the principal, your parents, or a special teacher. Share the problem with that adult and tell him or her why you suspect it.

Maybe your friend has given you some hints, implied that she was abused, or come out and told you, making you promise not to tell. You *must* break that promise, and she will thank you in the end. Perhaps she will have to be taken out of her home, and the law may prosecute the adult who has done the abusing, but remember, you are the link to your friend's health, well-being, and possibly her life. You are her link to hope.

Often an abused teen drops hints because she wants someone to know. She may feel the abuse is her own fault, and she wouldn't know how to go to an adult herself. An abusive adult usually convinces the young person that she caused this to happen, that his actions are normal, that everyone does it, and that if the young person tells, she will regret it the rest of her life. But abuse is never caused by the frightened victim. Never!

Go seek help for your friend. If the first person won't listen to you, go to someone else. If need be, go to your abused friend and tell her what you have done. Explain that you have talked to an adult and you want her to, too. Or the adult you have confided in may talk directly to your friend.

But whatever you do, get your friend the help she needs. Pray about it and act!

My friend just found out that she's pregnant, and she's considering an abortion. What can I tell her?

This is a crisis in which your friend needs a good friend to stand by her. How you respond may be a big help to her—or a hindrance. Whatever happens, you must decide to remain her friend and help her find the counseling she needs.

1. Begin by listening carefully. Show your friendship by offering her two open ears and an open heart. Don't try to solve her problem before you have listened to her entire story. The time to advise is later.

2. Once the initial shock has passed, help her realize the importance of making good decisions. Many people will want to tell her what to do, and the confusion could overwhelm her. Stand by your friend to help her make a decision she need not regret for a lifetime.

3. Get her to a good Christian counselor. There she can learn of the options she'll never hear about at the places that lead teens toward abortions.

Those who encourage her to end the life of her child will never tell her about post-abortion trauma. For the rest of her life she could wonder what that child could have been. Would he have been a scientist who discovered the cure for cancer? Could she have made great contributions to the world of art or written a book that would help thousands? What would the child have looked like? The questions are endless. Help her avoid the guilt and pain of abortion by getting her to someone who will provide her with many positive opinions. The most convenient way out will not provide a simple solution to all her problems. Remind her that clinics that perform abortion seldom, if ever, let a woman hear the heartbeat of her unborn child inside her. That's no choice.

4. Encourage her to tell her family. Naturally you will not want to do this if she comes from an abusive family that does not have her best interests at heart, but otherwise you need to encourage her to tell her mom and dad. She may fear that, but they need to have some input in this decision.

Imagine if you were the mother, and your seventeen-year-old daughter had become pregnant. Wouldn't you want to help her choose? Wouldn't you want to be able to pray over it and help her consider the options for adoption or allowing you to raise the child yourself?

5. Encourage her to consider adoption. Compared to abortion, adoption is a loving option. Millions of loving couples who cannot have children would love to raise a baby in their fine homes. Why not give them the chance?

If her parents do not seem interested in your friend's having the child, do what you can to make certain they are aware of the alternatives. Do they know the good news about the counseling that is available and the bad news concerning abortion's effects? Making a decision is not easy, but it can only be done with *all* the information.

6. Stick by your friend. Don't abandon her, whatever happens. Let her know the healing love of Jesus Christ. Tell her about His forgiveness and love. Let her know that though she made a mistake, God wants to love her through it. He loves her and the child she carries. Show her that love by remaining her friend.

Remember, your friend will have to live with the decision for a lifetime. Help her make the right choice.

What do you have to say about so-called bad friends?

Here's a poem that I wrote when I recently broke my bonds with a friend who was leading me downhill.

Bad Friends

Some friends are good,
and some are bad.
I know because
of some I've had.

Friends are made for lots of fun,
but when it's over, said and done,
was the fun good,
or was it bad?
Did it make you happy
or make you sad?
Think of last night.
Now are you glad . . . ?

Do they like to cheat
or lie or steal?
When you hang with them
how do you feel?

Can you look yourself
in the eye,
or do you ask,
"Why did I
do this or that,
just for fun,
even though it hurt someone?"

Is sex their thing
or drugs or booze?
How do you feel
from what you choose?

If you regret
the things you do,
then that should be
your biggest clue
to break the bonds
of friends who lead
you into pride
or sin or greed.

And if they keep
on doing wrong,
it's time for you
to say, "So long."

And yes, you'll have
two tear-filled eyes.
But please don't ever
compromise.

For who you are
is what you'll be
now and through all
eternity.

Please be wise, don't compromise.
Be smart, don't start.
Use your head, don't end up dead.
If you must say no, do so.

'Cause you'll be happy in the end,
If you break the bonds of
bad friends.

What's wrong with going to parties where alcohol and other drugs are offered? After all, I always say no. Can't I just go to be with my friends?

You *can* go to be with your friends, but are you wise to? Look at the chances you are taking.

1. You will gain the reputation of a drug abuser. Merely being around these friends puts you in their crowd and labels you with their reputation—drug user and abuser.

2. The crowd is stronger than you are. I don't think anyone can go to such parties over an extended period of time and continually say no.

A man had a beautiful bird who knew over fifty songs. When he planned to go on vacation for two weeks, he took his priceless, unique bird to a friend, who raised common, everday sparrows. He gave the friend careful directions on feeding and watering and everything else. His so-called friend said he'd follow the rules to the letter.

As soon as the songbird's owner left, the friend took the bird and placed him in the cage with his 100 common sparrows. He thought, *My friend is gone, and he will never know, so I will put the songbird in with my sparrows, and in two weeks' time it will teach my sparrows how to say more than "chirp, chirp, chirp."*

When the man came back, took his bird home, and removed the cover from the songbird's cage, it could only imitate the sparrows' "chirp, chirp, chirp."

The crowd will bring you down. I have heard story after story of teens who have gone to such parties, bringing along their own soft drinks. But in almost all cases, in a while those young people ended up drinking and using drugs. Don't think you can hang around people who use drugs and not take on their character qualities. If you won't, why do you have to stay around them? If you want to be popular with a group, it shows you really want their reputation.

3. You could suffer the legal consequences. If your friends get caught, you, too, could be arrested and prosecuted. Having charges filed against you merely because you were there is not worth it.

Why take the chance of being guilty by association?

4. You may have bad memories. If someone at the party dies or another crime takes place (besides using drugs), you will have the memory of it for a long time. The pain is not worth it.

Be smart, don't even start going to such parties. Choose new friends who will not drag you down.

5
Where Does the War on Drugs Start?

Do you think America should legalize drugs? I hear people say that if we made drugs legal, we would have less crime and that the drug war is lost anyway. What do you think? I am really confused!

To me, those who say the war on drugs is lost, so we should seek new ideas and legalize drugs, do not believe in hope for the hopeless. They don't believe we can meet any challenge or that we can clear up an evil such as drugs. They have a terminally negative attitude.

The day we legalize something we seem unable to control, we give up our power, creativity, and ability to do something about wrong. Drugs are wrong: They hurt and kill many people.

USA Today interviewed William Bennett, who headed America's war on drugs. He made some good points I would like to share with you.

1. Legalizing drugs would bring about more tragedies. More cocaine babies would be born, wrecking many more lives and tearing families apart. Teenagers would still run away and turn to drugs and prostitution. Legalize drugs and you multiply hurts. Airplane crashes, bus and train accidents would all increase.

Mr. Bennett pointed out that legalizing drugs would be legitimizing them. The number of abusers would rise sharply. Look back on the increase in alcoholics, after Prohibition was repealed, and you can see what we could have with drugs. Legalizing alcohol doesn't make it a helpful thing in a person's life, and it doesn't make it any less addictive. The law can never lessen the number of alcoholics, abused children, or broken homes.

If we legalized drugs, instead of 10 to 15 million users, we would have 50 to 75 million. Yet some still try to argue, "If we did it, people could make more intelligent decisions." Circumstances have proved that people don't always make the most logical choice. Look at the use of seat belts. Before it became mandatory, people often didn't wear them (and some still don't), despite overwhelming proof that they save lives. If we want people to live through car accidents, why not encourage them to stay away from drugs, which can be even more deadly?

Look at some other countries that have legalized drugs. Their tragedies have increased. Legalizing drugs can never solve the problem.

2. Drug legalization wouldn't keep us from destruction. When *USA Today* asked if legalizing drugs would destroy the wealth and power of the underworld, Mr. Bennett pointed out that if drugs were made legal, the United States government would buy and distribute them. They would have to deal with the drug lords in Colombia, since they could hardly expect Colombian president Barco to legalize them.

Look at the price America would pay. Drugs—possibly crack or cocaine—would become so cheap that sixth graders would be able to buy them the way they buy candy today. Put it within the price range of young people, Mr. Bennett pointed out, and they *will* buy it. By legalizing drugs, we could quickly bring about our own destruction.

3. Legalizing drugs is not the way to pay for drug education. When *USA Today* asked if drug legalization would not improve the funds for drug education, prevention, and treatment, Mr. Bennett pointed out that you'd surely need those, because America would have 50 million users.

If we *did* legalize drugs, we'd have so many people strung out that it would be a full-time job to take care of them.

Nor can we avoid the violence of a drug war by legalizing drugs. Today's drug lords will not want to lose control of their profitable territory, and they will not give up calmly. Accepting drugs by law will not lead us to a peaceful existence.

Mr. Bennett stands up for right when he says no to drugs. Whether or not we pass a law, right remains right, and wrong is still wrong. Making drugs legal will never change that moral truth.

The drug war hasn't been won, and it won't be until young people like you and parents like yours and people like me stand up against it. We need to speak out against drug abuse wherever we can. When a speaker tells you to find ways to party without drugs, and other teens snicker and laugh, do you have the courage to say, "Don't you realize that drugs kill, and people who sell drugs don't care whom they kill or hurt?"

Until we get angry at people who sell teens alcohol (the number-one cause of teen deaths) and other illegal drugs, we can never win this war. Until we realize that some people love money more than they love other people, we cannot make a dent in the armor of the underworld.

Legalizing drugs won't solve anything!

I'm always hearing that alcohol is dangerous. Why do people say that? What can it do to me?

How alcohol affects a person depends on several factors, including his weight, how much food is in his stomach, his emotional outlook, and the situation he is in (including the stress he is under). What doesn't do much to him may have a stronger influence on his girlfriend, who weighs less or may be having some emotional storms that make her vulnerable. The number of beers you drink is not the only issue.

Once you drink, the alcohol begins to travel through your system—especially to your brain. You'll know something has changed as these things happen:

1. You begin to feel relaxed. But before you relax, realize that your system is actually getting numb.

2. You begin to lose control. The alcohol begins to make you lose coordination and mental control. That's why you'll see a drunk who has trouble walking or one who slurs her words.

3. The alcohol takes over. The initial feelings of happiness and energy give way to confusion and loss of motor control; you can lose consciousness and even go into a coma. Sounds like fun, doesn't it?

4. Long-term effects take place. The more you drink, the more you increase your chances of health and mental problems. You may have increased trouble socially, too.

Physically, you increase your chances of:

Cancer (liver, stomach, mouth, or throat)
Cirrhosis of the liver
Weakened muscles or bones
Pancreas disorders
Heart disease
Permanent brain damage (including loss of memory)
Hallucinations

Emotionally and socially, you can increase the opportunities for:

Mental and emotional problems
Anger
Abusive behavior
Loss of friends
Loss of job
Increased sexual activity because of loss of judgment skills
Getting in trouble with the law or involved in a serious crime

Can anyone honestly say drinking is worth all that? Does it sound as much fun to get drunk anymore?

What's wrong with drinking beer? It relaxes me, helps me open up to people, and lets me talk more freely. Besides, I don't do it every day.

If you are a teenager and the legal age in your state is twenty-one, when you drink, you break the law. Despite such laws, many people—adults and teens—have the idea that underage people can drink responsibly. That just doesn't make sense.

If you can drink responsibly, when the law says no, you can responsibly shoplift on weekends. Can you imagine a parent saying, "Just steal the small stuff, Son. Nothing big. Only what you need, and never on Sundays"? How can anyone *responsibly* break the law?

Saying that beer relaxes you is crazy. Sure it does: It's a downer. It gets people depressed. Do you really want depression as a life-style? If you think I'm exaggerating, ask an alcoholic. His life is one of depression. He probably also got started by drinking beer.

When you need something to relax you, try something that's not addictive and destroying thousands of brain cells every time you put it in your body. Why not read something inspirational—like the Book of Proverbs or the Psalms? Why not plan to help someone? When you make contact with those who have more troubles than you, you can appreciate what you have.

You say alcohol helps you open up and talk more freely. What kind of talking are you doing? Many people become loud and boisterous and even start fights. Sometimes people even lose their lives in the arguments. Is it worth it?

Though you say you don't drink every day, how often *do* you drink? I have yet to meet an alcoholic who said, "I planned on becoming an alcoholic. I followed a carefully thought out strategy, and it worked perfectly." No, each alcoholic starts one drink at a time and never counts the cost.

Recently a high-school student sent Ann Landers a list of statistics from SADD (Students Against Drunk Driving):

Alcohol is involved in:
    66% of fatal accidents
    70% of all murders
    41% of assaults
    53% of fire deaths
    50% of rapes
    60% of sex crimes against children
    60% of child abuse
    56% of fights and assaults in homes
    37% of suicides
    55% of all arrests
    36% of pedestrian accidents
    22% of home accidents
    45% of drownings
    50% of skiing accidents
    More admissions to mental hospitals than any other cause
    50% of traffic accidents each year—more than 25,000 people

In addition, alcohol is the number-one killer of people under twenty-five years of age. These are sad facts, aren't they? But they *are* facts.

It amazes me that when I speak, young people all over this country stand firm and speak out in favor of the alcohol industry. They shout their favorite beer slogans and wear clothes that advertise for the alcohol companies. What the teens don't think about is that while they make the company executives rich, these people don't care how many homes are broken, lives are wasted, how many children are abused, or how many people are arrested for crimes committed under alcohol's influence. The company executives never warn teens that these things might happen.

The next time you see someone rich and famous singing about his favorite beer, realize that he's doing it for money. Notice, too, that he has been chosen to appeal to teenagers or younger children. Yet the executives of alcohol companies deny that they try to appeal to a younger audience!

I challenge you to find one person who has been drinking for a number of years and can honestly say it was a wise decision. She may talk about the fun or the wild times, but can she really say it was *wise*? Can he really say it has improved his life?

There is too much at stake to drink that beer!

If you really think drinking makes you feel more confident, ask yourself, *Would I want a brain surgeon to take a few drinks before he took a scalpel to me?* I think you have your answer.

Why are you so against responsible use of alcohol? If someone's going to drink anyway, what's wrong with a designated driver?

Certainly I will not encourage you to drink and drive. However, I'd like to suggest that you make an even wiser decision than having a friend drive: Don't drink.

I have five reasons for saying that.

1. It's illegal for teens to drink. Since when do you get to choose which laws to break? Having a sober driver does not make the drunk teens in his car any more legal.

2. Encouraging teens to drink lowers everyone's expectations. Instead of calling teens to strive for excellence, those who allow them to drink encourage compromise. Advocates of a teen's right to drink say, "Well, they will drink anyway, so we may as well give up our standards." They ignore the negative results of drinking on a teen's life and reputation.

I have more faith in young people. I believe they can live a responsible, alcohol-free, happy life.

3. We have lost moral standards. In allowing drinking, we have stopped calling right, right, and wrong, wrong. By saying teens can drink as long as they don't get behind the wheel, we give them a mixed message. They can no longer understand that teen drinking is wrong—and adult drinking isn't smart.

4. This attitude encourages teens to do "little" wrongs. When we okay "responsible use," we give them the idea that some wrong things are more wrong than others. That would be like trying to limit a teen's shoplifting—you still haven't dealt with the problem.

5. It gives young people a false view of popularity. By encouraging teens to "drink responsibly," we give them the impression that popularity wins out over the safety of our future— today's teens.

Plenty of people—even some youth speakers—will recommend responsible use and designated drivers. They do it for popularity's sake. Although these people don't make waves, they also don't challenge the teens they speak to to be their best. They don't want to sound "religious." But really, not drinking doesn't have anything to do with church—only with what is right.

Why don't people realize how dangerous alcohol is, when it's the leading cause of death for many age groups, not just teens?

We live in a society that has legalized alcohol for anyone who is of age. You'll see it everywhere, and even though it is an addictive drug, because alcohol has become so familiar, many people don't consider it one. Certain business or religious groups, families, and social circles find drinking perfectly acceptable. Many colleges and universities would not have a full enrollment, without the "attractions" of alcohol.

You'll see athletes and superstars selling alcohol on TV, radio, billboards, and during every kind of sporting event. They send the message that it's good to drink.

There are some specific reasons, though, why people become so involved with alcohol that they'd rather risk their lives—and the lives of others—than give it up:

1. Money: Businesses make millions of dollars from alcohol sales, from the companies that produce and the stores that sell it to the advertising firms that come up with the catchy slogans and promotions that make you aware of certain brands. Cigarette advertising has been banned from TV and radio, but alcohol ads appear on both media. Strong lobbying groups have the money to keep their "rights" to keep the ads there.

2. Addictions: Millions of people have become addicted to alcohol. This disease stays with people for a lifetime. Why don't people give it up? Because they know they are dependent upon their beer, wine, or whatever, and they don't want to make the effort to change.

3. Ours is a pleasure-seeking society. Americans are addicted to having fun at all costs—even death. Each drink gives a person a high, even though later he has a "crash" from the fun. Yet he'll continue to drink, despite the message his body tries to send him.

4. People accept drinking. "We've always had a few beers. What can it hurt?" a parent may say. "I'd rather have my kids drinking than doing those drugs." But that dad doesn't have a clue to the pain and suffering he could see in his children, when they become as addicted to alcohol as any drug user does to his drug.

5. Change is hard. Let's not kid ourselves. It's nearly impossible for some people to *consider* change, let alone change! Habits are hard to break, and it's easier to ignore alcohol than it is to confront it and revamp a life-style.

As I'm writing this, I'm flying from Milwaukee to Kansas City. The flight attendant just asked me if I wanted a complimentary glass of wine with my meal. I hope she didn't offer any to the pilot!

One night, while my friends and I were using marijuana and booze, we almost died in a car accident. I want to stop using them, but I know I'm weak. How can I say no?

It sounds as if you are afraid you can't say no the next time a friend offers you drugs or booze, and that concerns me.

In many cases, a teen who misses death by inches takes it for granted, once he recovers from the shock. In a short while, he may brush it off, without benefiting from the experience. I don't want you to be like that, and I'm glad you realize the seriousness of the situation.

Do your friends understand what happened? Are they stunned by the experience, or have they already gone back to their old ways? If they have not thought this through, maybe you need to make new friends who will not encourage you to take such risks.

When someone tempts you to drink or use drugs, remember that you almost *died!* Isn't that enough to make you carry through on your promise to yourself not to become involved in these things? Face it: If you do it again, you might not be here.

I'm glad you recognize your weakness. Now that you know it's hard to stop, take steps to combat your weakness. Seek out professional help, if necessary (and it may well be). A counselor can guide you in finding solutions and helping you become a stronger, more determined person. Take whatever steps you need to. Your life is more important than your desire for drugs.

I hope it doesn't take the death of one of your friends to prove the dangers of using drugs—*especially* when you drive.

Take a stand, get off the fence. You have good reason to hate drugs and what they do. Those who sell drugs only care about making more money and serving their own addictions—they *don't* care about you. Say no—a million times, no! No more for me. Never again. Period.

How can I help my school become drug free?

Take thirteen steps toward helping your school eliminate drugs:

1. Start with yourself. Make certain *you* do not use drugs, or you will never have much impact on your environment. Avoid all illegal and addicting drugs—that includes alcohol and tobacco.

2. Encourage others. Ask students, teachers, and everyone else in school to live drug free.

3. Get support at home. Challenge your parents to set a good example. Though alcohol, cigarettes, and caffeine may be legal for them, ask them to give them up. Why do they need those to get through the day?

4. Take the pledge. Once you have the approval of the school (which may offer you some good ideas), start a group of students, administrators, and parents who pledge to stay away from drugs. Remember, alcohol and tobacco are addictive drugs.

5. Ask for community support. Businesses or community members may be willing to donate TVs, stereos, videos, and so on to give away at drug-free activities students attend. They may also provide financial support or publicity.

6. Tell younger students. Get drug-free students to tell their stories to the elementary grades. Those who speak this way will raise their own self-confidence and reach other people at the same time.

7. Bring in drug-free speakers. Outside motivational speakers can often awaken an entire school to what drugs really are and what using them means.

8. Help students build self-esteem. Encourage programs that will raise students' self-worth. When that becomes healthy and positive, they will become less likely to ruin themselves with destructive elements.

9. Let former drug users share their testimonies. Invite people who have recovered from drug addiction to share their stories in classes. Let a former alcoholic describe what it is like to be addicted to drinking.

10. Promote drug-free activities. Have fun and wholesome times at drug-free parties, bowling, tennis, or racquetball events, a game night, skits, and so on. Get creative. I put strobe lights on my kites, and my whole family flies them at night.

11. Develop publicity. Start some fund-raising activities that the whole community can become involved in. Use your connections in the community to gain support.

12. Advertise the danger of illegal drugs. Make your student body aware that drugs ruin and never build up. They make dreams die. Help people to hate illegal use of drugs.

13. Seek help from community groups. Contact religious groups and law-enforcement agencies for support.

I know several kids who sell drugs to other students. I want them out of our town, but I'm no narc. How can I help?

Obviously you are aware that these people damage your town, or you wouldn't have asked this question. Friendly and popular as they may be, drug pushers ruin the lives of teens.

In order to stop this, become a silent stoolie—or a positive narc. You know who sells the drugs, and you know whose homes hold the parties with booze and other drugs. Call the police anonymously, or confidentially share the information with someone who will hold back your name. Get your parents' support and help. Many students have banded together to tell the authorities anonymously, and they have wiped out drug use. Because they cared, these teens have seen that people with addictions received help. You can do it, too.

When President Bush said, ''I will find you. I will catch you. We will prosecute you if you are using and selling drugs,'' he meant it. But he can only do that if Americans smell the stench of drugs in their own communities and decide to do something to eradicate it.

You don't have to walk through your school's halls shouting,

"I did it. I'm the one! I'm going to single-handedly clean up this town." Do it privately. Go to someone you can trust. Once you have brought it to his attention, it is his responsibility. He must make certain those using drugs get stopped and receive the proper help.

Here are a few quick suggestions about how you can make your environment drug free:

- Develop a twenty-four-hour phone line that teens can call to report where illegal drugs are being used or sold.
- Create drug-free activities for teens to take part in on weekends. (Remember, alcohol is a drug, too, so that means no drinking, either.)
- Start a drug-free club. Allow teens who are serious about quitting or those who will pledge never to start to join the club.
- If you know that someone is planning on a booze party, report it.
- Let the authorities know which parents make their houses available for drug or booze parties.
- Tell the police about stores that sell booze to minors.
- Encourage the police to set up "check stations," to catch drunk drivers in your town. Have them start in the parking lots of your town's bars on a Saturday night.
- Get the police, parents, your school, and the business community involved in encouraging teens to become drug free. Make it a total community effort.
- Become aware of the counseling available for teens in your community. Encourage drug abusers or drinkers to seek it.
- Avoid parties where people use drugs.

You are wise in wanting to clean up this problem. If a fellow teen or an adult would sell drugs in *your* school, he would sell the same drugs to your five-year-old brother or sister.

I'm glad the drug scene bothers you. Many people walk right by the locker where drugs are sold, or they pass by the alley where young people get their drugs, and they never open their mouths.

I applaud you for being silent no longer.

Do you know anything about Alcoholics Anonymous? I think I may need their help.

Yes, I do know about this organization. Though I have never been involved in it, I know it is one of the most respected groups that helps people fight alcoholism.

The basis of the ideas used in Alcoholics Anonymous is the Twelve Steps. Here they are:

1. We admitted that we were powerless over alcohol—that our lives had become unmanageable.
2. Came to believe that a Power greater than ourselves could restore us to sanity.
3. Made a decision to turn our will and our lives over to the care and direction of God as we understood Him.
4. Made a searching and fearless moral inventory of ourselves.
5. Admitted to God, to ourselves, and to another human being the exact nature of our wrongs.

6. Were entirely ready to have God remove all these defects of character.

7. Humbly asked Him to remove our shortcomings.

8. Made a list of all persons we had harmed, and became willing to make amends to them all.

9. Made direct amends to such people wherever possible, except when to do so would injure them or others.

10. Continued to take personal inventory and when we were wrong promptly admitted it.

11. Sought through prayer and meditation to improve our conscious contact with God as we understood Him, praying only for knowledge of His will for us and the power to carry that out.

12. Having had a spiritual awakening as the result of these steps, we tried to carry this message to alcoholics, and to practice these principles in all our affairs.

The Twelve Steps are reprinted with permission of Alcoholics Anonymous World Services, Inc. Permission to reprint the Twelve Steps does not mean that AA has reviewed or approved the contents of this publication, nor that AA agrees with the views expressed herein. AA is a program of recovery from alcoholism. Use of the Twelve Steps in connection with programs and activities which are patterned after AA but which address other problems does not imply otherwise.

In addition, Alcoholics Anonymous has these slogans to help you through life. Let them encourage you:

"Let go and let God—we do our best and leave the results to Him."

"Easy does it—change takes time."

"Live and let live—what's right for us won't always be right for someone else."

"Together we can make it—it's O.K. to lean on others sometimes."

"How important is it? People are more important than things."

"One day at a time—every day is a new beginning. It can be whatever you make of it."

"First things first—most important of all is God's will."

"Keep it simple—work on one thing at a time and not take on too much."

"Listen and learn—it doesn't hurt to listen."

Notice that the Twelve Steps deal not only with the alcohol and the powerlessness of the alcoholic, but with the unmanageableness of the alcoholic's life and the belief that a Power greater than the alcoholic could restore him or her. That Power is God.

Alcoholics Anonymous reaches out to people of all faiths, so the steps describe God "as we understood Him." I challenge you to read the Bible, which says only one God exists, and you can only get to Him through Jesus Christ, His Son. You can follow the steps of AA and recover from alcoholism by believing in a greater power than yourself, but you don't get to heaven that way.

I want you to recover from your alcoholism, but I also want you to go to heaven, because you will die someday, and your eternal life will depend on your decision about Jesus. Believe in Him, through His guidebook, the Bible, and you will spend eternity in the presence of the holy, loving God. Reject Him, and you will spend it in the torments of hell.

Contact AA. People there will respond in love and in the strictest confidence. Their commitment factor goes like this: If you ever need help in the middle of the night, when you think you might take another drink, call someone from Alcoholics Anonymous, and a person will come to be with you and talk you out of it.

Look into AA; it could help you for the rest of your earthly life. Also accept Jesus, who can give you eternal life.

One of my parents is an alcoholic. I hate alcohol because of the pain it has brought my family—we used to be so close. I have so much anger bottled up inside. Where can I get help?

Families with an addicted parent have an unwritten "no talk" rule. Whether the parent abuses alcohol or drugs, this rule says, "Thou shalt not talk about the addict's behavior or let anyone else know about it."

Alcoholism or drug abuse breaks up the family's balance. No one can play a normal role, so instead of being a father, mother, son, or daughter, each takes on a secret role or identity. The more a family member upholds the no-talk rule, the unhealthier his or her role becomes.

Look at your family. Which of the following five roles have you taken on? What has a brother, sister, or the nonabusing parent become? (Keep in mind that any of these roles can be played by either sex.)

1. The *chief enabler* experiences feelings of guilt, anger, pain, fear, and hurt. He accepts and provides responsibility. He blames himself and becomes too serious. By taking on the role of su-

perresponsible person, he becomes caught up in self-pity. The chief enabler is fragile and manipulative. He feels the abuse must be his fault. The person who plays this role must realize it is dangerous and may affect him the rest of his life.

2. The *family hero* feels inadequate, confused, hurt, and lonely. She has built a wall of defense around herself. Providing self-worth and pride for the family system becomes her main role, so she seeks success. If she can be really successful, she rationalizes, perhaps no one will notice Mom or Dad's drinking problem. While she seems to have it all together, she works hard for approval from anyone and everyone. She acts special and superresponsible. Often she develops an independent life, away from the family, to take the focus from the problem drinker or drug user.

The problem with this role is that the family hero never thinks she can be real or have hurts. She needs to get counseling and return to a normal role.

3. The *mascot,* or *joker,* provides the family with fun or humor. When he feels fear, confusion, loneliness, or insecurity, he becomes louder and funnier. Though he jokes a lot, he is fragile inside. Often he becomes so hyperactive that people wonder if something is wrong or if this is who he really is. He will do anything to attract attention, because he loves people. While he makes others laugh, he cries inside. Fear and insecurity grip him.

4. The *scapegoat* tries to distract the focus of the family system. She feels hurt, rejected, angry, lonely, and may develop an unplanned pregnancy or become a substance abuser herself. As a defense she may become totally withdrawn or act out her pain in a crime. She may become defiant and close to her peers.

Don't become a scapegoat. The abuse is not your fault, but your parent's problem. Your mom or dad needs help. Don't cover up your feelings or think this role will reduce your fear.

5. The *lost child* offers relief. Though he feels the same emotions as the others, he covers them up by being very quiet. You never know where this distant person is or what he thinks. He might become superindependent, while he totally withdraws.

Lost children may become overweight or have an eating disorder, such as anorexia or bulimia. Quite often their line of defense includes rejecting others. This quietness does not remove the pain; it only makes the problem worse.

I don't know which role you play, but whatever it is, get the counseling help you need. The longer you encourage the no-talk rule, the longer your parent's disease goes on. While you cover up the truth, nothing will change. Members of the family need to break this rule so the drinker or drug user can get at his or her true feelings and end the family secret.

Will it take an overdose, an accident, or a family disturbance to make you act? You can get out of your role now. Seek professional help. Organizations and support groups, such as those connected to Alcoholics Anonymous, may help you. Often they are free of charge. Find people who have walked in your shoes and know how to climb the mountain and get away from the defensive role-playing situation.

It's time to talk.

6
How Can I Help Others?

You talk about being a leader, not a follower. How do I know if I am a leader?

Leaders have the following characteristics:

They contribute to their classes, families, and schools.
They are always part of helping, not hurting.
Instead of tearing down others, they build them up.
While others start fights, they settle differences.
They are in control of themselves.
They care for others.
They walk their talk.
They are not bossy, so people can look to them for creative solutions to their problems.
They know right from wrong.
They ask questions, without fearing those who might call them dumb.
They stand up for the less fortunate.
They have great compassion for the hurting.

They usually believe in causes more than their own enjoyment.

How many of these qualities do you have?

I'd like to tell you about one leader. A couple of years ago, Josh McDowell, who has spoken to more college and high-school students than anyone else alive, invited about 100 speakers to be part of his "Why Wait?" weekend retreat, in California. He taught us creative ways to show teens why they should wait until marriage to have sex.

We all arrived at the retreat site in a twenty-hour period. Guess who carried most of our bags to our rooms? Not the bellboy, but the man who had a million things on his mind that would make the conference a success—Josh McDowell.

Now that's leadership!

Guess where Josh McDowell got his idea of leadership from in the first place? The answer is the same one you'd give to the question, "Who washed His followers' feet about two thousand years ago?" You've got it: *Jesus!*

Being a leader means being a servant. If a person has too much self-importance to serve others, he or she is no leader. That means you do dishes and clean your room before you clean up your town.

Leadership doesn't mean you wash your dad's feet, but it may mean you help wash his car. How can you wash your little brother's feet? (That's a weird thought, isn't it?) Maybe you do it by being nice or at least not trying to get even. Though being nice to your brother may seem like a radical thought, I think it's what Jesus had in mind.

I know someone who is hurting, but he won't tell me what the problem is. How can I help him open up?

You cannot force anyone to share with you, but you can open the door, gently and quietly. Begin by following these guidelines:

1. Develop an icebreaker. When a professional counselor first sees a family, he may have a parent share all the problems she has with the child. After Mom lists the sixty-nine things John has done wrong, the counselor turns to the child and says, "I bet you're delighted to be here today, aren't you? You probably couldn't wait to get out of school and rush in here with your mom, so she could tell me about these things you do to upset the family life."

If that doesn't raise a chuckle or let the child know the counselor is open to his side, he might add, "It's tough raising parents today, isn't it?"

When you counsel with a person, you, too, need to let him know things are not one-sided. Build up some hope. Perhaps you can have the teen answer the question, "What things would your mom or dad say are wrong with you?" After the teen lists five or six things, bring in creative humor to show him there is some hope. Get him to laugh and realize the moment will pass.

2. Ask him to define the problem as he sees it. More than likely this will be very different from Mom or Dad's point of view.

3. Encourage him to seek possible solutions to the problem. Ask what he has tried in the past. Make a list of things that have and haven't worked. The more clearly the person you counsel sees his problem on paper, the easier he will find it to understand. In addition he will be able to see that he *can* get through this.

4. Offer additional counseling. You may discover that another counselor could better help this person. Maybe you know someone who has lived through his problem and has discovered steps that work. Don't be afraid to refer him, if you know more help is available.

I know I need help, but I just can't seem to tell anyone. How can I develop the courage to ask others for it?

No matter what problem you have, sooner or later you will have to deal with it. You can wait, and the problem may get worse, or you can tackle it now, while it's smaller.

By admitting that you have a problem, you have already shown wisdom, but you need to take action. Begin by focusing on the fact that talking about your problem will get it out in the open, where you can deal with it. Don't put your eyes on the difficulty of speaking, but on the benefits that may result from sharing your trouble. Find solutions, people, ideas, encouragement, and hope. You don't have to live in the middle of something that's too big to deal with alone. Learn to live free from worries. Get help!

I'm concerned about someone. I know he is hurting, but how can I approach him so he won't take it the wrong way? He hasn't

let me help before, but things seem to be getting worse.

The fact that you want to help your friend shows you have feelings, empathy, and a desire to help. Those are all good. They will help you as you try to give this friend a hand.

Here are some other things to remember.

1. Chances are that your friend is crying out for help. He just doesn't know how to express his need. Put yourself in his place. What has it been like to hurt in your own life? How have others helped you? You seem willing to help him now.

2. You may be the only person who can feel his hidden pain. Don't let fear keep you from becoming part of the solution. Later he may thank you for taking that first step.

3. You could wait too long. Don't let his story be part of the daily news; then it will be too late. He shouldn't have to slit his wrists before anyone has the courage to offer help. Go to him. If you feel uncomfortable doing it alone, find someone who can help you, and go together.

I know what it's like to be in that kind of situation. Several years ago I waited too long to help a friend whom I knew was hurting. He hanged himself, and to this day I regret not acting on the intuition that told me to help him.

You can't help someone who will not let you. If he still remains closed up, you cannot push him. But leave him with the message that he can turn to you if he changes his mind.

If the situation seems impossible, keep these guidelines in mind:

1. If he will not share with you, leave him with hope. Share the truth that there is an answer to every problem. Give him some reason to believe that life can become better.

2. You may need to share the need. If you have reason to believe this is a life-threatening or extremely harmful situation, go to an adult and tell what you know. Don't carry too heavy a burden on your own shoulders. *Do not* spread the news around among your friends. You are not a trained counselor—get help.

3. Pray for him. If you know you can do nothing more, still pray for your friend. God can reach the places no human can. Even though he may not turn to you again, your friend may find the help he desperately needs. God has everything in hand when we have lost control.

A girl came to me for help, but her problem is too big for me to handle. What should I do? Should I tell her to come back later or send her to someone else?

When someone comes to you with a problem that you cannot provide counsel for, don't simply tell her to come back, unless by doing that you will be able to provide the help she needs. Instead stick with her until you can connect her with others who *can* provide assistance.

Even if you can't solve all her problems, you can still help her by:

1. Listening. Show her that you care enough to be there when she needs you, to listen without interruption, to concentrate on and understand what she says. Listen to her the way you would like someone to listen to you when you have a problem. Don't jump in with possible solutions before she has finished telling the story. *Listening* means "open ears, close mouth."

2. Admitting your limitations. If you can't provide counsel, don't fear admitting it. Let her know, though, that you can put her in touch with someone who will help her.

3. Contacting another counselor. Take her to an older, wiser person—a school counselor, a caring teacher, or someone trained to find an answer.

By taking these steps, you will let her know her situation is not hopeless. Together with caring counselors, you can find an answer.

How can I convince people I will keep their stories and problems confidential, if they share them with me?

Are you a peer listener or just a friend who wants to help others? If you are a friend, follow these guidelines:

1. Don't be a blabbermouth. If you spread a person's troubles all over school, no one will want to share with you. After all, you wouldn't want an embarrassing story about you to become public knowledge. How much less a person with a serious problem wants it known.

2. Earn the trust of others. Even if you don't have a reputation for talking about others' problems, you need to let them know you will be openhearted and trustworthy. Until your friends know you won't broadcast anything and that you will not be overly judgmental, they will not feel secure.

3. Know when you've reached your limits. As a friend, you can offer an ear. Listen carefully and support the other person, but do not provide advice when the situation has gone beyond a friend's control. Instead refer your friend to a trained counselor who can provide in-depth help. By listening, you have done right, but you cannot solve everything alone.

If you are a peer listener, the above truths are for you, but so are a few more.

1. Understand your school's policy. Know what you can and cannot do. Adults should have set the rules, and counselors and trained professionals should provide advice. Abide by their guidelines.

2. Keep things confidential. The confidentiality rule is twice as important for a peer counselor. Only discuss a person's problems with your adult advisor and possibly another peer counselor, if he or she needs to know something. *Never* share such problems with your friends. Even the most juicy story should remain in confidence—remember, your talking could have serious consequences for the person who shared the problem.

3. Know when to break confidentiality. Whenever you counsel someone, begin with this rule: I will keep everything confidential, unless it means you or someone else would be at risk in the situation—in danger of abuse or suicide. If you must break confidentiality, tell only a trusted counselor who can help the situation.

If you become trustworthy, people will open up to you. Strive to keep these effective-counseling rules.

I want to become a peer listener and help other teens. How can I convince the rest of the school—or even just a few kids—that I can help and that I can help them?

Is there a peer counseling program in your school? If so, join it; if not, you may want to help start one. However, you will need the cooperation of your school, in order to do it there. Establish a good relationship with the administration, teachers, and the proper professionals. Their backup becomes essential if you run into problems you cannot handle. Do not seek to do it with students alone.

1. Begin by getting the proper training. Once you have done this, let other students know you are a peer listener and have been trained to listen and initiate help.

2. When you start, gain small successes. Help those with small problems first, to gain some background. Don't take on the largest problem in your school, because failure at that may stop you in your tracks.

3. Ask the school what problems they most need help with.

Form a committee of adults and students; put out a survey to find out where the student body needs you most. Let your school know you are for real and that there is hope. You can be part of the solution to hopelessness among your peers.

Forming a peer-counseling network or becoming part of an established counseling team may not be easy, but stick with it. You'll want to convince students that you have an answer they may not have found elsewhere. Above all, remember you are a listener, not a trained counselor.

Why do you feel our country has so many problems? As you travel around the country, have you seen things that might cause them?

No one answer covers everything, but we have to realize that people are free to make choices. That's how God made us: We can chose Him or evil. With sin come the consequences and pain.

Here are a few results of our inclination to sin instead of turning to God.

1. God has become a joke to millions of people. Though they remain unwilling to obey God's laws, they expect God to love them endlessly and uncritically. By taking away the consequences of sin, they avoid confronting what He says about judgment. But that won't last forever—look at what the Bible has to say about judgment day and the land of fire, in the Book of Revelation.

2. We have no respect for life. We treat people like things and things like people. Though we'll spend millions of dollars saving the whale, we spend just as much on legally murdering unborn babies. Though we cry for the seals and become passionate over the shooting of a bald eagle, we try to remain uninvolved in the abortion issue.

3. We take over as creator and God. If a person has a terrible disease, doctors may "help" by injecting poison into her system. We create "perfect" babies in a test tube, but destroy those who have identifiable problems. In one state parents sue the doctor who has not saved the life of their child, while in another, parents sue the doctor who made it possible for their handicapped child to live.

4. Families aren't forever. At the drop of a hat, people get divorced. As soon as "the feeling is gone" they want the right to "try again."

5. Instead of what *is* right, people focus on "peoples' rights." Look at the way we treat others:

- Women want the right to do what they want with their bodies, so their unborn children die.
- Prayer in school offends one person, so we take it out of every public school.
- In the name of the "right of privacy," a civil-rights organization fights to allow teens to use drugs and alcohol and still remain on the team.
- Because someone misread him his rights, a convicted rapist and murderer goes free to rape and kill again.
- When a child has been sexually abused, an adult's lawyer has the right to publicly drag that youngster through the horrible memories, all in the name of justice.

Standing up for rights means standing up for right, but until America learns it, we will go on to worse and worse wrongdoing. Where will it end?

6. Because we compromise so much, we are confused. Look at the mixed messages we give teenagers:

- We tell them, "Don't drink and drive," even though underage drinking is illegal.
- We encourage them to have "safe sex," but never talk about the dangers of having sex outside marriage.
- Neighbors who would call the police if they saw someone stealing a hubcap will ignore a party at the house down the road, where 400 teens drink and then drive.

7. God blesses us, and we become incurably selfish. Look at it in our life-styles:

- God gives us an abundance of food, and we overeat. Then we have to spend our time jogging to take the pounds off. Meanwhile, people in other lands starve.
- We ignore the elderly while we pursue our hobbies and play with our toys.

To turn America around, we have to change our priorities and attitudes. Only by turning back to God and His laws will we have a truly peaceful nation.

To make changes in our nation, we need to do it one person at a time. Begin with yourself. How do you need to change your attitudes and actions? Start with your own life. Then ask God to show you ways you can begin to lead friends and classmates into a closer relationship with God and better values in their lives.

7
How Can I Have a Home, Sweet Home?

Everywhere I look, I see broken homes and families falling apart. Why are they crumbling around us? What can we do to avoid it?

Keeping families together is a job for each and every person. Here are six steps we can take:

1. Make family life a priority. The family is the basic cornerstone of society, and if it fails, so will neighborhoods, cities, and our society. It is happening all around us.

Families are important. If we put God in first place, families next, and ourselves third, we would have successful family lives. We need to stand up against people who don't support family values.

2. Understand that human beings *are* important. The individuals who make up the family are created in God's image. We need to show others that an eight-month-old fetus is a human and an old, helpless person is not nonproductive and therefore something we can throw away. People are of vital importance.

3. Look out for others. In a world that says, "If it feels good, do it," most people think individuals are more important than families. When parents rush after their careers and desert the family, they leave homelife in the dust. We must look out for the individuals in our families.

4. Turn time crunches into time priorities. Everyone gets busy doing something. Mom and Dad go to work, and the kids become involved in a million activities. No one has time for the home. Realize that you can spend time doing many good things, but you need to set goals and decide what is important. Each person has a real need for the structure of the family—on it rest self-esteem, jobs, and future families.

5. Take divorce out of the picture. America has made divorce too commonplace and easy. If the current husband or wife doesn't seem to work out, someone will advise you, "Get out. You don't have to put up with this." Marriage is a lifetime commitment. Unlike most of today's dating processes, it should never be easy come, easy go. Make your dating pattern one that nurtures a relationship and creates a life mate.

6. Make God part of your family. Going to church is fine, but putting God in first place is another thing. Make God a living, vital part of each family member's life. When you stand up for Him at work or school, you may receive a tremendous amount of ridicule, but making God number one will be worth it—it enhances your whole life.

Why does an underprivileged family sometimes have a happier homelife than a more privileged one?

When you ask this question, are you assuming that *money* means "privilege"? I hope not, because if you are, you couldn't be farther from the truth, when it comes to family life.

Some families have lots of money. But to make the high income they enjoy, Mom and Dad spend extra hours in the office. They come home so tired they can't even love, nurture, and have fun with their children. Though they may not realize it, their push for success creates an underprivileged family, because all the money in the world cannot make their children happy.

In other homes, with lower incomes, Mom and Dad spend time with the kids. They get to know one another and make father, mother, brother, and sister more important than possessions. I openly and wholeheartedly applaud them.

Family members *decide* to create privileged homes by giving family life an important place in their days, setting group goals, developing traditions, and spending creative time together. Their life together draws them closer. As a result members have less stress. They usually avoid alcohol or drug problems, abuse, and other destructive situations.

The child whose Mom and Dad take him to church, pray with him, and teach him how to relate well to others belongs to the truly privileged family—no matter what income bracket they belong to.

Why don't my parents listen to me?

When you can't seem to get through to Mom and Dad, ask yourself, *How is our communication?* Believe it or not, your parents probably *want* to know what you think. Yet they may not know where to start, so give them a hand.

To talk to Mom or Dad successfully, first, make sure that you choose a good time. If Mom has just heard that her sister is very ill, unless yours is a serious problem and you need an answer immediately, you'll do better to talk later. If Dad's trying to keep the sink from overflowing, and you want to talk about going to the baseball game, he probably can't give you much attention.

That doesn't mean you shouldn't arrange a time to talk or that you should allow an overbusy parent to get away with never speaking to you. Just make certain you haven't chosen a bad moment.

Once you have Mom or Dad's attention, ask yourself the following questions:

1. Am I listening to my parents and taking their advice to heart? If you ask them what to do and then always ignore their advice, before long your parents will feel you didn't really want their input at all. They will respect you much more if they know you have taken their words to heart. Seek deep inside yourself to see if you are really looking to them for answers and guidance. Do you treat them the way you would like to be treated, if *you* were the parent?

2. Am I willing to behave toward my parents the way I want them to behave toward me? You want to go to a dance, but your parents object, because they say they don't want you coming home late. If you respond in anger, don't expect Mom and Dad to remain cool and calm. You can't reserve the exclusive right to express that emotion.

3. Am I behaving in a know-it-all fashion? If you are, your parents will probably close their minds to your suggestions. They want you to benefit from the lessons they have learned, instead of making their mistakes all over. In most cases, no one, outside of God, loves you as much as they do. When you treat their advice as if you value it, they become more apt to listen to you.

After a friend has listened to you, you also listen back, when he needs help. You confide in people who confide in you and respect those who respect you. It's the same with your parents. Treat them the way you'd like to be treated, and you will open new lines of communication. They *will* listen, if you don't act as if you already know everything.

4. Do I remain calm when we discuss important issues? If you don't immediately agree, don't get hot under the collar. Listen carefully, to make certain you understand what your parents mean. Don't jump to conclusions and burst out with a harsh reply.

5. Do I keep my word? Let your parents know you will keep your end of any bargain. Get home by your curfew; treat your car with respect; take care of your room; treat your brothers and sisters well, and so on. By doing these, you will gain their respect and build up the trust level that makes good communication possible.

You advise lots of teens to write letters to their parents, when they have a problem. Why is this better than talking it out?

If you have open communication with your parents, you may not need to write a letter to them. That's great! But in many families and situations, that kind of communication does not exist. Writing a letter may help people understand one another and set up good lines of communication.

If you're having trouble reaching or understanding your parents, write a letter. For these reasons:

1. A letter lets you speak your piece. Usually, when parents and teens have problems, they have a hard time talking without shouting, interrupting one another, or fighting. Writing can help you get all your ideas down, without interruption or emotional flare-ups. Your letter can get things out in the open by identifying the problem and your feelings.

When your parents read the letter, they can each do it as a person, not a parent. They cannot scream or get angry, because you won't be there to hear it. Since you know these things, you can feel free to fully express yourself.

2. A letter helps you plan what you want to say. Before you write, think about what you want to communicate. You may want to:

(a) Tell your parents how much you love and appreciate them. Focus on these positive emotions as much as possible.

(b) Share the things you've enjoyed with them: times spent working together; the closeness you've had; special family feelings; the ways you've cared about one another; traditions you love; and times spent wrestling, hugging, reading, or having special quiet times together.

(c) Then tell your side of the story. Explain how you see the problem. For example, if you think they don't spend enough time with you, tell them.

When you write, pick your words especially carefully in this part. Could you be misunderstood? Are you attacking them? You want to open communication channels. Don't make bitter or inflammatory remarks. Remain humble. Never throw things in your parents' faces. Remember, written words can be remembered long after spoken words have gone. Don't write something you may regret. Be gentle and loving and kind; it may pay you in big dividends in the future.

(d) Suggest some solutions. What are you willing to do to help the situation? What do you want your parents to do? Ask yourself, *Are my expectations realistic?* Tell your parents you need their wisdom and experience. Never act as if you have all the solutions.

(e) In your planning, you may decide to write separate letters to each parent. You may have special words for your mom or things you need to say to Dad. By writing two letters, you may communicate better.

(f) Pray about your letter. Make certain what you say will please God. A nasty-sounding letter will not make Him happy. One that is caring and kind will.

(g) Prepare to spend a lot of time on this. It is more important than any term paper you will write. By doing it well, you will invest in your relationship with your parents. Your time will be well worth it.

(h) When you are done planning, write the letter in a rough draft. Then let an unbiased, trusted adult go over it. An older, wiser person can help you with the finishing touches, tell you if something is hard to understand, or let you know if you sound angry or diplomatic.

3. A letter can start better communication. Remember, though, this is not a cure-all. Don't expect one letter to make everything perfect or completely change your mom and dad. We are all creatures of habit, and it's hard to change, but it's a start.

I hope you don't need to write a letter to your parents, but if you do, try it. From there you may go on to being able to talk things out—it could be a good start.

My mother has me under lock and key. She's so worried that I'll get pregnant or do drugs. How can I gain her trust?

Correcting a situation like this means you have to do some hard thinking and work. Here are steps that can help.

1. Take a good look at the past. Have you done anything that made her distrust you? Did you lie and get into trouble? Was there some misunderstanding between you that you need to correct?

Maybe it isn't really you. Did your mom get in trouble when she was your age? If so, she may be trying to help you by saving you the pain she felt. Does she have trouble trusting people in general? That can spill over onto you.

2. Take a good look at yourself. Ask, *Can I be trusted? Do I lie to Mom or manipulate others? Do I honor my parents and desire to obey them?* Look at your positive and negative points.

Next ask, *Why should I be trusted?* Write out your answers.

3. Make up a plan to gain your mom's trust. If you lost her faith because you lied, identify specific ways you can earn her trust. Work hard to show her how you've changed. You will have to put effort into earning what you've lost. Did your mom make a mistake when she was young? Then show her you are levelheaded enough to make wiser choices. Make her proud of you. If she has trouble trusting people, show her ways in which she can have faith in *you*. Misuse of the car made her doubt you? Prove to her you can drive like an adult. But don't think you can take her for one "safe ride," while you drive like a crazy with your pals. The first time a friend asks for a crash helmet before she'll get in the car with you, your mom will know it's all a hoax.

4. Write out the plan. Think of specific small areas you need to build trust in, and list them. Then identify larger areas for the future.

5. Share the list with your mom. Talk to her and tell her what you want to do. Together agree on a final plan you can put into action. The negotiating skills you learn here may last you a lifetime.

Even if you were not the untrustworthy person, it's hard to build up someone's faith in you. It may take time, so be patient. You can do it!

Why do parents do things that hurt kids instead of helping them?

I could draw many implications from your question, because adults can hurt teens in many ways. Let's try to zero in on a few.

1. They may do good things that hurt. If my daughter is grounded and says, "You're a mean father," that is the way she perceives me. She thinks I'm mean to discipline her, but I am really trying to help her.

Be careful how you look at things. Is your perception clear? What causes you pain may be something that could help you in the long run. Your parents might actually be doing you a favor.

2. They may react out of their own pain. If your mom or dad had trouble in the past that has never been resolved, he or she may respond out of anger. Such a reaction can blast right through a teen.

I have seen this in teachers who have unhealed pains; their reactions to students may be coated with the hurt in their lives.

Even if they don't mean to harm anyone, they can. If someone does this to you, understand that he may need healing even more than you do. Forgive him, pray for him, and reach out a helping hand to him.

3. They may cause pain unintentionally. I believe that most parents do not plan to hurt their teens. They love them deeply, because they have brought them into the world and have hurt and laughed with them. Some loving parents still pass personal hurt and confusion along to their teens. If your parents have this kind of life, talk to a trusted adult who can help heal those hurts.

4. They may need better communication. If you think your mom is not doing something that is good for you in the long run, talk to her. Before you open your mouth, though, try to look at your mom's actions as if you were the parent. Put aside the desire for instant gratification. Look at the big picture and see it from a different point of view. Then talk it over.

If you cannot talk to your mom, bring another adult with you—but only in an extreme case. First try to open communication channels yourself.

5. They may actually be abusing the teen. Yes, some parents *do* abuse children. They need professional help—immediately. No matter what threats have been given to you, the authorities should be contacted. Get help and tell someone. By doing that, you may save your own life.

My mother spends all her time with my younger, handicapped brother. She totally ignores me, except when she expects me to

**do things around the house. I have no so-
cial life at all, and she expects me to dress
old-fashioned. I'm dying inside. Where
can I turn?**

Yours is a very difficult and confusing situation. Let's try
to untangle it and provide a few strategies that will give you
hope.

Normally a mother will spend the most time with the child
who needs the most help. While she cares for your brother, she
probably does not realize that you need her, too. You need her
time and love, to have fun with her, to get to know her. I think
you must tell her that. If you can't talk to her, write her a letter;
that way interruptions or an emotional outburst won't distract
you. You can also finish your sentence before she says anything.

Tell your mother how much you admire her care for your
brother, but that you are handicapped, too, because you also have
burdens—it's as though you have no mother and many chores.

As you look back on the help you've given your mother during
these years, you will probably see that you've become a stronger
person because of it. The trials you've gone through have shaped
your character and prepared you for the future. But you have to
choose whether you will let the tough times and confusing situations build you up or tear you down. If you respond with anger
and bitterness, the pain will follow you until you free yourself
from those debilitating thoughts and emotions. But if you look to
God for strength and believe He is training you, the trials can
make you the kind of person you'd like to become.

I admire the fact that you have done so much extra to help your
mother, but don't let that burden ruin you. Can you imagine how

troubled and stressed your mother feels in this situation? She probably has done the best she can and does not know how to do it better. Forgive her for any ways in which she has hurt you, and let go of the anger. Ask her forgiveness for whatever you have done that has hurt her. Let healing begin.

I don't know why your mother encourages you to dress in old-fashioned clothes and have no social life. If you can share this with your mother, do so. If not, why not ask a counselor for help? Bring your mother to talk to a caring person who will help you both understand what is going on.

The attention your brother gets may even make you wish you were sick, so you could get attention, but I don't think you really want that. Count your blessings. Enjoy the fact that you have a future ahead of you in which you will have the abilities to live a normal life. Your brother will never do that.

Instead, learn how to have attention in positive ways. Help your mother know what you need. Seek God's blessing in the middle of the confusion and hurt.

My father stays at home all the time. He is afraid to leave the house, to answer the phone, or even to get out of bed in the morning. Quite often he won't even go out and get the mail until after dark. What can I do?

It sounds as if your father has many fears that keep him from acting in a normal way. You'll need to encourage him to see a psychologist or psychiatrist—or if he can't do that, encourage him to contact a support group. He may have *agoraphobia,* "a fear of being in public or open places," but a counselor will be able to diagnose him properly.

Many people call agoraphobia the fear of fear. Those who have it may be afraid of driving, going to church, using an escalator, or even walking through a mall. Usually a victim of it will have a panic attack while he is driving a car, and because he associates the attack with driving, he becomes afraid of doing that. While the attack is underway, he will feel as if he is going crazy or about to die. His heart pounds as if it could explode, because a surge of energy seems to be trying to break out of his body.

Does your dad make up excuses all the time to get out of being around people or going anywhere? If so, he probably is agoraphobic. His doctor may not even know about the problem, if your father won't talk about it or go to the doctor's office.

Depression and fear of losing control accompany this disorder. Don't ask your dad to go places with you or make him feel bad because he does not take part in your life the way other teens' parents do. Don't get upset when he won't take you places, because he is battling a terrible problem. To him, moving out of his comfort zone seems like the end of the world.

Contact a local counselor who will be able to help your dad. Ask about a support group. Your dad's life can return to normal, but it won't happen overnight. Many people who do recover say they feel glad to be living again, but they may always struggle a bit with the problem.

Help your dad to find help. He needs to understand that God made him special—just the way he is—and that no matter how he feels about himself, God sent His Son to die for him. Let him know you love him, no matter what: Give him total, unconditional acceptance and love. Encourage other family members to understand his problem and not push him into groups—even around the holidays.

Encourage your father to seek caring professional help. Then pray for him, so that he will have the strength to get that help. Also pray that the Lord will help you have patience and the insight to understand your dad. Jesus, your Best Friend can make all things possible.

In this tough situation, keep caring about your dad!

My mother's live-in boyfriend has me concerned and confused. He acts friendly, but I don't trust him. What should I do?

Beware, you are in a potentially dangerous situation!

Any man who lives with a woman outside of marriage does not respect her. If he did, he would not involve her in such a harmful situation. Look at the impact it has on both parties:

- It drags your mother's self-worth down. Each time they sleep together, she feels more used and valueless.
- He shows her that he has no commitment to her. He can leave anytime he feels like it, if she doesn't do what he wants or expects. To keep him at her side, she always has to be certain she makes him happy—no matter what he asks of her.
- He causes her sin and shame. Much as some will try to tell you otherwise, people do not respect those whose life-style includes live-in boyfriends.

- They do not respect God's standards. God clearly tells us not to become involved in adultery. He will not be mocked and will deal justly with those who break His laws.

In addition, the situation is dangerous for you. If he respected you, this man would court your mother and ask her to marry him. By living with her, he shows he has no moral foundations or integrity. He does what pleases him. If the right moment presented itself, he might decide to seek his kicks with you, as well. A great majority of sexual-abuse cases reported concerning children and teens involve someone close to them or who lives in their house.

Don't do anything to lead him on: Be careful how you act around him and see that you don't spend time alone with him. If you get an intuitive feeling that this man has his eye on you, get away. Go to live with your father, if you can. If that's not possible, seek other help, through a counselor or an adult you trust. If no one listens, keep on trying until you find a safe way out. Follow your gut reaction and *always* protect yourself.

My mom is a single parent. I know she has problems, and I'd like to help her. What advice do you give to single parents and their teens?

First, I'd like to applaud each single parent for doing the job of two people all alone. Raising a teen is tough enough when you share the job; I can't imagine raising my kids without the help of my wife!

I also feel I should apologize to single parents. Quite often they get treated as second-class citizens. Not too many places have activities for them. Even many churches don't seem to want Mom without Dad or Dad without Mom.

When I talk to single parents, I give them this advice:

1. Don't be a single parent anymore. Let God help. Give Him your worries, fears, stresses, and frustrations. Turn to Him for guidance and hope. Read His Word and understand His plan for your life.

2. Don't bad-mouth your ex-spouse. Remember, the person you divorced or lost is your child's parent. That's something you cannot change, and speaking badly of your spouse will never help your child.

3. Raise your own self-worth. By doing this, you will show your teen that a person can feel good about himself in a tough situation. Remember, all things are possible with Jesus' help. Time heals a lot.

4. Develop a positive attitude. When you face a problem, tell yourself, *If this is as bad as it gets, I can make it.* Look back on past successes, to remind you of the things you have come through well. When problems arise, say, "No problem"; chances are, once you change your attitude, it won't be.

5. Pray with your kids. Daily get on your knees and look to the Lord with your kids. Show them He still controls the universe—and your life.

6. Avoid a physical relationship until you remarry. By obeying God, even when it hurts, you will show your teens that God's rules apply to you, too. Don't do one thing and expect your teens to do another. By abiding by His rules, you will encourage your teens to wait until they marry to have sex.

7. Enjoy your kids. Do fun things with them as often as you can. Get weird and wacky, and you will both benefit from it.

Share those points with your mom. When you can, help her to make them possible.

Now, here are some guidelines for you.

1. Help out as much as you can. This doesn't mean you have to stay at home all day, but go out of your way to support your mom around the house and do chores. Go beyond what she expects. By lending a hand, you will develop a deep, positive character that will stick with you forever.

2. Help emotionally. Be a listening ear, a hand to hold, and a friend. Let your mom tell you some of the frustrations and pains of being a single parent. Allow her the right to be a normal person, not a supermom. No one is indestructible.

3. Bring faith in God into your family. When the world starts to overcome you, God can offer relief. Pray with your mom and grow close to Him together. Worship together in church.

4. Don't feel ashamed of your mom. Be seen in public with her. Go shopping or to a movie together. By supporting her this way, you will give her a wonderful gift that won't cost you a cent.

5. Stay above the law. Don't do things that are wrong: drinking alcohol, driving too fast or recklessly, or involving yourself in problems at school. Those can wreck any family, but a single home is especially vulnerable.

If you go above and beyond what is expected, your future and your home will be happier. Invest now in your family!

My dad is remarrying, and I don't know how to deal with my stepmother. Any advice?

When either of your parents remarries, you can expect big-time changes in your family life. Part of the changes, though, are up to you. How will you respond? What kind of treatment can your stepmother expect?

As you wrestle with the new situation, do yourself a favor by keeping these things in mind:

1. Don't expect a stepparent to be like a biological parent. Your stepmother may try to fit right in—I hope she does—but she can never take the place of your real mother.

No matter what, still give her a fair shake. Let her get to know you, and don't expect her to take right over where your mother was. If you know she will be different, you may not object as much when she tries out new things or makes changes.

2. Accept her for who she is. No doubt your stepmother has many good—and bad—qualities, but accept her as she is. Make the most of her good points. Hopefully she will return the favor to you.

The new family life may hurt you, but your stepmother, too, has felt pain. Decide to go forward with God's help and create a new family, instead of remaining tied up in the past. If your parents have divorced, don't blame your stepmother for that. It will only make you and others miserable for a long time to come. Looking forward has many more benefits than turning back.

3. Take time to establish a relationship. Anything worthwhile takes time to build. Little steps in the right direction will lead to a good family life. So don't expect miracles overnight—or even within thirty days. Bonding may take several years; in the meantime, be friendly and courteous.

Give your stepmother the courtesy you would give to your dog. Even on a bad day, you'd pet him. When things are rough at school, you throw your Frisbee for your dog and feed him. If you kicked him every time something hurt, you wouldn't have that pup for long. Don't treat your stepmother that badly, either.

4. Look upon her as a friend, not a parent. At first you need to accept the fact that you could become friends. You might actually like each other. Maybe you can laugh together. Perhaps she's a better cook than your mom—so enjoy it! Seek out some common ground. Tell her what your favorite things are and give her a chance.

5. Don't become impatient. Things may not come as quickly as you want them to, but don't give up. Let things take their course, and build upon the good things that happen day by day.

6. Disregard your mom's opinion about your stepmother. If there's been a divorce, your mom is likely to feel hurt and angry. She may not be able to see your stepmother fairly. After all, she naturally sees your dad's remarriage as an insult to her, and that pain will take time to heal.

If your mother dwells on this subject, in a loving way ask her not to mention it again.

Live your life as freely as you can. Don't let the hurt and pain from your parents' broken marriage tear you apart. The way you live now, the words you say, and the thoughts you allow to fester or those you turn away will control your today and tomorrow. Give this relationship a chance.

7. Don't feel guilty. When you accept a stepparent, you may feel you have been disloyal to your mom, but you haven't. No one can really take her place.

You are merely growing in your world and giving it a chance. By treating your stepmother well, you can learn about compassion and understanding. You can make life beautiful again. If you decide to marry someday, you can build your marriage on a solid foundation.

No matter what, follow God's rules for living. Don't take all the pain out on your stepparent. Though a blended family isn't a simple situation, it can become wonderful. Make certain you survive: Give your stepmother a chance.

My father remarried, and he acts as if I don't even exist anymore. He won't talk to me, hug me, or care about my life. What can I do?

Whether your father is having troubles because he's adjusting to a new marriage partner or because as a teen his father didn't relate well to him, the chances are his attitude comes from overwhelming problems within him. Perhaps he would like to reach out to you, but just doesn't know how.

You can open the door to those feelings by taking these steps.

1. Write him a letter. Tell him how you feel, that you need and love him, that you want to have hugs and spend time with him.

2. Suggest family counseling. You all need to regroup and become friends and a family. Whatever the troubles, they need to be out in the open, where each of you can deal with them. If your dad won't go for counseling, seek it for yourself.

3. Make God a real part of your daily lives. Spend time in the Bible. Ask your dad if you can read through a book of the Bible together, discuss it, and ask, "How can this apply to our lives?" Make church a regular part of your week.

If your dad refuses to reach out to God, do these things on your own. Pray for him each day.

4. Forgive each other. Go to your father and ask him to forgive whatever wrongs you have done. Make certain you also forgive him for his mistakes and wrongdoing. Pray about this, before you go to him, so that you will confront him with a gentle, forgiving spirit.

5. Focus on the future. Things may not change overnight. You'll need to have patience. But you can have hope that God and caring counselors can lead you to a better tomorrow.

6. Avoid bitterness and anger. When things don't go as quickly as you'd like, or if you don't see any change in Dad, don't let these negative emotions control you. By allowing them in, you could spoil the rest of your life.

7. Keep trying. Don't give up. Leave notes to your dad, saying, "I love you." Reach out in many ways, even if you don't get much response. Let God guide your steps.

The effort you put into this will be worth it. Drawing your dad close to you is a good goal, one God has for you. Through it all He will give you strength, no matter what happens, if you rely on Him in all your ways.

My mom and dad are both alcoholics. How can I help them?

In such a difficult situation, it's good that you want to help your parents. Make the most of that desire by taking the following steps:

1. Help yourself first. Before you can effectively reach out to your parents, you will need support. Contact Alcoholics Anonymous and ask for information on their Alateen program (this organization helps the children of alcoholics). Become part of it, and you will be able to talk to others who face the same situation in their homes. Find out what helped them and how you can use these strategies in your family.

2. Don't take responsibility for your parents' problem. You did not make the decision to drink, though your mom and dad's choice has influenced you. False guilt can burden you until you feel so frustrated that you do not seek help, so don't let it start.

3. Break the "no talk" rule. Families try to hide alcoholism, because they feel ashamed and don't want others to know of the problem. Before you can stop the situation, you have to share with someone you trust. Get help now.

4. Realize your limitations. You cannot solve your parents' problem or make them go to Alcoholics Anonymous. You can only encourage them to become involved with the group and do the things they recommend. In the long run, whatever happens, remember that you don't have the job of cleaning this up.

5. Pray, pray, pray. You can't go this one alone, so make God your greatest Friend. Talk to Him about the problems you face. Ask Him to help your parents. Tell your parents you are praying for them.

Remember that God, who controls the universe, can change lives. He can help your mom and dad quit drinking. Turn to Him. Trust in Him.

6. Ask someone to help you call a family meeting. You need a chance to share with your family and come to some decisions.

When you meet, tell your parents how much you love them, and encourage them to give their all to counseling. Seek the support of others in your family. Breaking this addiction will place a strain on you all. Start from a point of strength.

7. Be as patient as possible. Alcoholism doesn't start in a moment, and it doesn't go away that quickly either. This disease lasts a lifetime. At first your parents may not even be willing to admit to the problem, but now more than ever they need your support. If you had the same problem, you'd want them to stick by you, wouldn't you? Love them the way you'd want to be loved—unconditionally. It's okay to hate the disease that has made them this way, but continue to love your parents, because that's what they are.

8. Become involved in counseling. Make every effort to take the time you need to go to it. Answer questions honestly and openly. Walking around with a chip on your shoulder will not help anyone stop drinking. Give your parents the help they need. Give it your best shot.

9. Decide that *you* will never drink. Because your parents have this problem, the odds are much greater that, if you *do* drink, you will become an alcoholic. I offer this simple advice to all the relatives of alcoholics: Don't ever drink!

10. Honor your mom and dad. God commands us to honor our parents, so make sure you respect yours. Let them continue to be your parents and feel that you need them. Ask them for their advice and help. Let them keep their dignity. They will need that in order to make a full recovery.

You need the help of others to overcome this problem: God, counselors, and friends. In the same way, your parents need your help. Don't give up.

8
What Can I Do When Home Isn't So Sweet?

Why do so many marriages end in divorce?

According to the statistics, one out of every two families will experience the pain of divorce. Yet those figures can't even begin to account for the multitude of broken hearts, confused minds, and bruised spirits that result from it.

How is a family torn apart? Each couple could tell a different story, and no one can make the pain disappear by slapping a Band-Aid on the family. However some hard truths frequently appear in broken families:

1. Relationships disintegrate over time. Usually one big problem will not cause a divorce, but when a lot of little difficulties build up over time, and the couple does not deal with them, they can find themselves in trouble. A man and woman must confront minor irritations or frustrations as they occur, or the two drift farther and farther apart. Often the straw that seems to break the camel's back has little to do with the real cause for the breakup.

2. Poor communication patterns cause poor marriages. Many experts label poor communication as the number-one cause for divorce, business failure, and bankruptcy. A bankrupt marriage ends in divorce.

To understand the need for communication, compare it to having a best friend. Would you expect your friend to stay around long if, every time he started to share a problem, you ignored him? Of course not! You wouldn't want to have a friend who never wanted to hear about your successes, either. Well, it's like that in a marriage, too. A husband and wife who do not share the happy things—and the sad things—can't be best friends. When a man or woman shuts out the other partner, it hurts. Before long, the warmth in the marriage begins to disappear—and so does the spouse.

To keep together, a husband and wife need to make caring communication a part of every day. They can write notes to each other; say "I love you," and mean it; send birthday cards to each other; and leave creative "I miss you" messages on the answering machine.

3. People can give in to the pressures of the world. Society's negative forces can squeeze out the caring, faithfulness, and love in a marriage. When friends or co-workers say, "It's okay to have sex outside of marriage. Go out and party, and do your own thing," an unsuspecting couple may try it. But those self-pleasing attitudes that promise so much fun pay off in long-term anxiety and hurt.

To ward off the pressures that can tear a family apart, instead of the world's advice, couples need a secure relationship with each other and with God.

4. Messed-up priorities cause big trouble. Many couples just take life one day at a time. They never set goals for the year or know what things are more important than others. As a result, they end up continually putting out fires, they expend most of their efforts in the wrong places.

When families put God first, their relationship second, and themselves third, they have found the formula for success. Couples in which each partner seeks pleasure before the mate's needs and leaves God out of the picture just don't add up. You can see it in their lives, because they'll have a hard time of it.

5. Lack of preparation is a trap. Many people never seek counseling before they marry. I recommend that an engaged couple seek out a professional counselor or a pastor who can give them four or five sessions in which they can learn what to expect. During this time they can think through upcoming issues such as money matters, vacations, in-laws, and so on.

A trained counselor will help the two think about and talk out areas that can become great frustrations, if they are not dealt with before the marriage vows. What personality differences could cause friction? How much of this attraction is based on sex? If people expect to keep a marriage alive on sex alone, they will surely land in the divorce courts. The average couple has sex less than ten minutes a week; what will they do with the rest of their time together? Counseling can help such people discover the things that can bond them together; or it may help them decide they could make better choices concerning marriage partners.

6. Time pressures can push out marriage. In our society, anxiety over time hinders many relationships. Too many things cram our lives, and we lack enough hours in the day to accomplish them. So we drive up to a window to grab a hamburger, deposit money in a bank, or care for many other basic needs. If someone stalls out in line in front of us, we honk the horn, yell, and generally show our anger.

You cannot build a strong marriage at a drive-up window. By flicking the button past thirty-seven television channels, we do not learn the communication arts that will last through the boring, hard-to-enjoy-each-other times. A successful marriage takes more than a moment.

7. An empty place in the God space won't hold a marriage together. Many families have completely lost or forgotten God's ideals. The place where God should fit in their hearts is empty.

How many homes have a sign on the wall that says, IN OUR HOUSE WE WILL FOLLOW THE LORD? Does the family have a special place where they can worship? Maybe they have a family Bible that measures twelve feet wide, six feet long, and a foot thick. But how deep is the dust on it? They may display it as an ornament, but can anyone open it?

Outward displays don't count for much. God needs to be alive in relationships—especially marriages.

8. There's no room for "safe sex" before marriage. When members of a couple have been free with sex in their dating relationships, after they marry each will compare that mate with earlier partners. If the husband or wife does not match up well, their relationship suffers. "Safe sex" before marriage will hold a person in bondage for years to come.

9. Looking into the past is part of the future. Before a person marries, he or she needs to ask, *What kind of relationship did my* *future spouse have with his or her parents?* Was Mom an alcoholic? Did Dad abuse her? What traumatic experiences from each person's past will affect the marriage? Engaged couples need to share them.

That doesn't mean that only perfect people, from perfect families, can marry; but if a partner needs counseling, it should take place *before* the wedding. Serious homework needs to go into any decision to marry.

God's plan is that each couple marries for a lifetime. I pray that when you marry, you will find the right mate and plan against divorce. Plan for mutual commitment and a lifetime of growing and glorifying your Creator together. When you marry someone whom you know loves God more than he or she loves you, you know your mate has a commitment to these ideals—and God's plans.

10. No one should marry "because we're in love." Getting married for love alone is a big mistake. After all, I love stunt-kite flying, yet I would never marry it.

Any couple who does not marry because they share common interests and because it is God's will will not make it. Starry-eyed love cannot last through the tough times.

While you date, ask yourself, *Does this relationship please God? Am I in His will in the way I date and react to this person? What do we have in common? What could we talk about in twenty years? Does he hate what I hate? Does she enjoy the things I enjoy?*

Before you marry, ask yourself, *Is it God's will that we marry?* If you're not sure, don't take that step.

I have yet to meet a husband or wife who planned, from the first, to get a divorce. However, I *have* met many who never planned not to. They never talked about and thought out these things; they never wrote out some ways they wanted to avoid such a breakup. When the tough times came, these unprepared people had nothing to rely on. Slowly and surely, their marriages fell apart.

How can I get my parents to stop their divorce?

There are no guarantees that you or anyone else will be able to stop your parents' divorce. The breakup of a marriage has many causes, and no one can expect a quick-fix answer to solve them. Counseling may help, but the only *real* cure for a divorce is that both parties want to please God and seek His will. Only His strength can help them turn aside from selfishness and lack of consideration for the other person, or money, personality problems, and other troubles.

No matter what happens to your parents, though, you can still have hope. You *can* keep your head and heart together and come out in one piece. Take the following steps.

1. Don't bury yourself in false guilt. *False guilt* means you take the blame for something you did not do. You did not decide to have your parents divorce, and you cannot take the blame for their actions. Neither could you have stopped it. Don't allow these bad feelings to overwhelm you.

2. Get counseling. Talk it out with a professional who can give you real help. Work through your hurts, anger, and confusion now, so they won't stay with you for life.

3. Expect to grieve. Just as if one of your parents had died, you can expect to feel deep sorrow over this loss. The hurt may go on for a long time. But realize, too, that time will ease the pain. Right now you can only think about your parents' divorce—it's the focus of your life. As time passes, you'll be able to focus on other, more positive things. If you do, you'll find that life's become less black.

4. Talk with friends or teen counselors whose parents divorced. If you know someone who has gone through it and come out successfully, ask his or her advice. Find out how that person coped. What helped? Will that work for you, too?

5. Spend time reading your Bible, every day. Look up God's promises to His people (those who believe in His Son, Jesus). Memorize verses that give you help. Hide them in your heart, and they will help you again when times get tough. When you focus your thoughts on what God has for you, you won't focus so much on pain.

6. Be around upbeat, positive teens who are a good influence. When you hurt, you do not have as much strength to stand up against the bad things. So make certain you spend your time with people who can help you think positively and keep you at your best. Avoid drugs, alcohol, and premarital sex. They don't provide you with the answers you need and will only bring you down.

7. Don't become bitter. Pray for the ability to forgive your parents. Realize they are hurting, too, no matter what they do or say. Good or bad, they are still your mom and dad, and they still need your love.

Though you have not caused the divorce, and you couldn't do much about it, you will hurt the most. At times you may feel like a yo-yo, swinging between your mom and dad. But there is still hope.

Trust God and develop a special relationship with Him. Draw closer to good friends and your parents. Others have lived through this horrible, scary situation, and so can you!

My parents are getting divorced, and I'm in the middle of a custody battle. When the judge asks me whom I want to live with, what can I say?

When I get a letter like this one, I always wish the teen behind it didn't have to deal with such a hard situation. How can anyone choose between two parents, hurting one and for a short time making the other happy? I'm no expert on this, but as I've talked with young people, they've shared their insight.

Begin by asking yourself:

1. Do I understand that it isn't fair? You shouldn't have to choose between your parents, and it won't be an easy decision. No matter what you do, you can't completely win. Make the best choice you can, and leave the regrets behind.

178

Take many things into account. Maybe one parent cannot support you, or one has abused you. A choice like that seems easy. It's harder when you have two parents who love you and want you to live with them. Or what if you have two equally bad choices? Take it to God in prayer and look as objectively at the situation as possible.

Once you've made the decision, leave it in God's hands. Torturing yourself with guilt will never solve your problems.

2. Whom do I feel comfortable with? If you had to decide which parent you get along with best, which would you choose? Do you fight with your mom and have peace with Dad?

Realize, too, that the old saying "Opposites attract" has some truth to it. If you have a perfectionistic dad, and you are easy-going, it could be difficult—but you could also offset each other's strengths and weaknesses. Perhaps you could help Dad lighten up, and he could help you get organized. Go into this, though, expecting a few rough spots.

3. Which parent am I closest to? Do you have a special bond with Mom or Dad? If all else is equal, you may decide to go with the one with whom you experience the most love and with whom that special closeness seems to last longest.

4. Which would cause the least upset in my life? Would you have to change schools, leave your friends, or move to another state? Think carefully about this important factor. Would you have a lower stress level, because you'd experience less change, if you moved in with Mom?

5. Which parent allows the most contact with extended family? I think it's important to keep as much of your support system intact as possible. Grandparents, aunts and uncles, cousins and nieces and nephews can provide security in the midst of change. If moving in with Mom would take you across the country from your family, you may decide to visit Mom and live with Dad. A few weeks at a time across country could be better than a whole life there.

6. Which one is more stable? Could one parent bring the influence of drugs into your life? Does one have few emotional resources? Which environment will give you the best chance to cope with life and develop positive character qualities? If you need help with this decision, perhaps you should talk to family friends and ask their opinion.

7. Which parent has the closest relationship with God? If one of my parents knew Jesus as Savior and would root me in a strong church and help me spiritually, I'd probably choose that one. That's not to say that the Christian parent will *always* be the right choice. Some Christians don't act tactfully; they hate everyone, after the divorce, and avoid church altogether. God has given you a mind and common sense. Use these assets when you make this important decision. You don't need a parent who has a lot of anger at God to keep you down now.

8. Which parent would demand the most of me and give me the best supervision? We all feel safer when we have a parent who is strong enough to say no when we want to go to the wrong place, with the wrong crowd, or into the wrong situation. Studies show that teachers and parents who have healthy enough self-worths to set limits on a teen's actions are preferred by those teens.

Consider the parent who will challenge you to do what's right and not just give in when you yell long and loudly.

By asking you to make this decision, the judge places you in the middle of a vise; it gets tighter, no matter what. You'll be squeezed, no matter whom you choose. Pray long and hard. Ask the opinion of many trusted individuals who know your family. Pray again for guidance, and see what God says to your heart. Only by letting Him show you the way can you win.

My parents are getting a divorce, and my dad says I'm to blame for it. What can I do?

Though it's normal and natural for you to feel as if you have caused your parents' troubles, *you* are not the cause of your parents' breakup. Because you badly want to keep the family together, you may feel guilt, but many things go into a divorce, and a child cannot cause any of them.

When you think back to the fights, disturbances, or stressful times, realize that these came out of deeper problems between your parents. You may never know what those troubles were, but you can overcome their results.

Your parents' divorce *will* cause you problems and confusion. As you face them, remember:

1. Your mom and dad chose to get the divorce. Divorces take place for a million and one different reasons. But your parents made the bad decisions in their relationship—you did not. Neither could you choose to get the divorce—they alone could make that decision. You did not make the mistakes, so yours is not the blame. Though the hurt and pain don't leave you, the blame must—for your emotions' sake.

2. Your parents probably feel very angry right now. The emotions that accompany a divorce are very powerful, and they tend to overflow into every other part of life. Your dad's accusation comes out of that emotion, and he was probably really taking out his anger at your mom on you. Though it wasn't right of him to blame you, he probably didn't really mean what he said. Don't let words spoken in a loud, out-of-control moment ruin your relationship for a lifetime.

3. You are not alone. Others have felt the pain of divorce and know what it's like. Learn from them how you can have a better life. Don't fall into the "poor me's"; discover how you can make positive decisions. Seek out counseling that can help you put things in a better perspective.

4. How you respond is up to you. You can seek out the positive or wallow in the negative. What your parents have decided *will* strongly influence your life, but it doesn't need to have full control.

For example, you can choose to forgive your mom and dad. Though it may seem impossible, with God's strength, you can do this thing that you know is right. He will help you respond in love, not bitterness. Remember, a bad situation can make you bitter or better. Choose a better way.

Try to become a positive source for Mom and Dad. You have to *choose* the right path.

5. Turn to your Best Friend—Jesus. God certainly doesn't want your parents to divorce—His Word tells us that. But even in the worst situations, He wants to have you close to Him. When everything looks totally impossible and out of control, He has not become powerless. Hold on to Him in faith, and He will bring you through.

Life isn't always easy, but it isn't hopeless, either. Yes, you are in a bad situation, but you don't have to throw in the towel. You do that when you take the blame for something you never did. Don't take the responsibility for sins you never committed—instead accept the love of God.

How can I get my divorced parents to at least talk to each other and stop putting each other down in front of me?

When parents divorce, it may be as if you'd been thrown into a war zone. Though their pain may have existed before, now it swells forth in a wave of bad words and attitudes.

You have no guarantees that you will be able to reconcile your parents. Some divorced people cannot forget the deep hurt and pain that come when a marriage self-destructs. However, keep trying to influence the healing process. The situation is not impossible.

First, realize what is going on behind your parents' words and closed doors of communication.

1. Your mom and dad are not really angry with you. Though they say terrible things, you are not their target. Together they have accumulated a lot of hurts that still linger. The harsh things they say are not arrows meant to pierce your heart, even when it feels that way. Like two-year-olds who are throwing a tantrum, your parents allow their emotions to have control, instead of taking control of themselves.

2. They have closed the doors on each other. Because they cannot communicate without hurting each other, your mom and dad shut each other out. To try to end the pain, each may simply act as if the other did not exist. Though that doesn't solve the problem it makes it more bearable in the short run. Before they can open communication, they need to begin to forgive and understand the pain.

3. Your mom and dad need your love. Though they may never tell you so, now more than ever they need to know you still care deeply for them. Life has become uncertain, because of the divorce. It's a time when they need all the love they can get.

4. Each fears you will side with the other. Your mom may fear that your dad will tell you something that would make you hate her, so she may tell you about what your dad has done—or she may hit you with a cloud of vague accusations about how he mistreated her. To make certain you don't get the idea your mom is Ms. Perfect, your dad may tell you some things *she's* done wrong—even if you'd rather not hear it.

5. Their situation needs healing. No matter how self-assured your mom and dad may seem, apart from the harsh words, their attitudes show that they need to have healing in their lives. The words and closed doors reveal their need to forgive each other—and that's hard.

Trying to get people together under such circumstances may seem as great a task as bringing peace to the Middle East. At times you may feel as if the political situation is easier than the battle in your home. It may be tough, but don't give up. Instead, use these guidelines for bringing peace:

1. Accept the fact that healing may take time. Don't encourage your parents to put off seeking healing, but also do not expect that they will change overnight. As you seek to bring peace, be grateful for the small victories, even though you may see little overall progress.

2. Love each of your parents unconditionally. No matter what happens, they need your love. Tell them you love them, but don't stop there. Show your love in practical ways. Do things that will help them understand your feelings.

3. Forgive your parents. When they say awful things about each other, you may have trouble forgiving them. When you hear of a wrong one has done against the other, sometimes it's harder to forgive than if it had been done to you. Ask God to help you forgive—holding on to grudges will do you no good at all.

4. Pray for your parents. Though you may not know all that went into the divorce, God does. Ask Him to work in their lives, to bring reconciliation. He alone can bring the peace they seek.

5. Write two letters to your parents, one for each. Tell them how much you need them and love them. Explain how you feel when they attack each other. Paint a vivid word picture of how it makes you feel inside.

As you write, tell them that you will not stop loving them. Be certain you are gentle with your wording, because you are dealing with a very painful place in their lives. Do not condemn them or attempt to make them feel guilty; they already feel bad enough. Just show them how you feel.

If you can, share your letters with an unbiased adult who cares for you. You do not wish to say anything that could cause more hurt, and an adult may be able to point out things that will improve your letter.

6. Encourage good communication. Your parents may never communicate easily, but you can make certain *you* keep the doors open between you and your mom and you and your dad. Even when they cannot speak to each other, be certain *you* keep clear channels. Though it's not an ideal situation, you can still have their love.

7. Be careful what you say. Since they are hurting, don't play one parent against the other. Don't intentionally make Mom feel guilty by telling her of a wonderful thing Dad did with you. It will be like pouring oil on flames.

At the same time, don't let your parents drag you into saying awful things about them. Maybe you can't choose how they react to each other, but you can decide how *you* will act. Make your words wise and gentle by asking God to guide you.

Making peace in a family is not easy. It takes time, patience, and persistence, but don't give up. Jesus has this word for you: ''Blessed are the peacemakers, for they will be called sons of

God'' (Matthew 5:9). If you love Him and seek to bring peace, you are acting as God's child. What greater blessing can He give?

My mom and dad are divorced and don't get along at all. How can I help them understand that I need them both equally in my life?

Let your parents know how much you need them. Tell them in person, or if you cannot, write them a letter. Do you have a reason why you can't talk or write to your parents? Then ask another adult to explain it to them. Don't let anything stop you. Communicate. Tell Mom and Dad that no matter how old you are or how independent you seem, you need them desperately.

At the same time, try to understand what your parents are going through. If they have only just gotten divorced, they are probably reacting out of deep emotional pain. Perhaps they can't control their feelings. Disbelief that this happened engulfs them. A lot of confusion, anger, and so on have made it impossible for them to think straight. When they hurt so much, it's hard for them to realize that you have problems and need them.

If you have a big fight with a friend and go home, only to have one of your younger brothers or sisters ask you to play a game, you feel as if that's the last thing you could do. *How juvenile!* you might think. The same kind of stress influences your parents, if they have just gone through a divorce. Pray for them and help them where possible.

Have your parents been divorced for a while? If they never settled these emotional strains, they may still have problems getting along. They need your prayers more than ever. Forgiveness, for themselves and each other, can heal them.

Because of all their problems, your parents may not be there for you. When Satan gets his way and overwhelms us with hate, instead of love, he fills us with the desire for selfish enjoyment instead of commitment to our families.

Your hurt is real. Once divorce comes into your life, you need the strength and support of others. Turn to God, friends, and wiser people who have successfully walked along this path. Though life may seem scary and dark at the moment, it does not have to stay that way. It can become beautiful again, once you get out of this valley. Seek the strength for this journey!

A little while ago I wrote the following poem that I plan to use to end every speech I make to teens this year. Because it gives you a capsule version of my message, I'd like it to be the last thing you read in my book, too:

Sing the Right Song

What does it mean to know right from wrong
And have the courage to sing the right song?

To do your own thing, not follow the rest,
By looking ahead while they cheat on the test.

And Saturday night will I follow the crowd,
By getting drunk and rowdy and mean and loud?

Will I steal if it's easy or lie if it's cool
And in the end become the fool?

Or will I be smart and do what is right
And to my convictions hold on tight?

I'll ask myself this every day
Or from the truth I know I'll sway.

What does it mean to know right from wrong,
And have the courage to sing the right song?

There's a campaign that says, "Don't drink and drive:
We want our kids to come back alive."

But they forgot one thing, I saw,
For teens to drink is against the law!

It's sad when we stop being wise
And from absolutes we compromise.

A boozer on the corner, Friday night;
We pull down the shades and turn off the light.

Call the cops? You're kidding! I don't get involved.
Besides, what do you think would ever be solved?

Oh, I'd call them if you stole my car,
But selling liquor to kids in my favorite bar?

What's the big deal? You're so uptight,
Getting raped at a party is not my fight.

What does it mean to know right from wrong
And have the courage to sing the right song?

But it is our fight, and it's a Great Big Deal!
If someone's selling drugs, I'm gonna squeal.

I'm sick and tired of lies and thugs
And families ripped apart because of drugs.

And the way they teach there is no God
And if you must, it's okay to rob.

And sex can't wait, the desire's too strong;
Dr. Ruth is the leader of this loud song.

They tell you to abstain, but before you go,
They say use a condom if you can't say "no."

They can say it all day long,
But that doesn't make it any less wrong.

Right is right, like the rising sun;
Don't let your ethics come all undone.

What does it mean to know right from wrong
And have the courage to sing the right song?

Our kids are asking from deep inside,
"Isn't there anyone with any more pride?"

Adults are too busy on their jobs all day
to call up their kids to talk and say,

"Just because it's cool, doesn't mean you do it;
And if it's not good, I will put a stop to it."

We need dads to stand and lead this fight,
To love their children and teach what's right.

And moms to shout, "Enough's enough,
No matter what it takes, we're gonna be tough."

And teachers to walk hand in hand
And lead our kids across this land.

And there is a God, so bow your head;
You're alive right now, but soon you'll be dead.

So remember:

If it's wrong, then do something about it;
And if you know it's right, then go ahead and shout it.

And never stop asking all night long,
What does it mean to know right from wrong,
And have the courage to sing the right song?

My prayer for you is that you "Sing the Right Song"!
Then you can handle life, sex, and everything in between.

If you have any questions, problems, or answers you would like to share with me, please drop me a note at:

Bill Sanders
P.O. Box 711
Portage, MI 49081

If you have accepted Jesus as a result of reading this book, we have some materials we would like to send you. Please fill out the following form and send it to me at the above address.

Name: _____

Address: _____

City: _____ State: _____ Zip: _____

Personal story (optional): _____

_____

_____

_____